Beach Chairs and Baseball Bats

A Celebration of the
Cape Cod Baseball League

by
Steve Weissman

To Randy #
Sandi ~
See you at
the Ballyard!

Text design, cover design, and title page art by Andrea LaFrance

Photos are copyright Steven B. Weissman except where otherwise noted.

Front cover photo of Ben Copeland, Harwich Mariners, courtesy Bob Prew

Back cover image of old-time Wareham players courtesy Dan Dunn Collectables

Mr. Weissman welcomes inquiries, comments, and requests for speaking engagements. Please email him at steve.weissman@theballyard.com for more information and to be informed of any future offerings.

ISBN 1-4196-0508-9

This book is dedicated to the spirit of Terrence Mann, Crash Davis, Joe Hardy, Dottie Hinson, Roy Hobbs, Bingo Long, Jake Taylor, and every other character – fictional or living – for whom baseball is so much more than a game.

Table of Contents

Introduction

Dear Reader:

My first experience with the Cape Cod Baseball League took the form of a chance encounter in Chatham in 1989, when on a misty summer evening, my fiancée and I happened upon a well-lighted field upon which stood nine young men with "A's" scripted on their shirts. Fortunately for me, Andrea is as big a baseball nut as I am – imagine finding a girl who once worked as a vendor outside Fenway Park! – so we placed our dinner plans on hold and picked out a place in the bleachers.

We weren't quite sure what we were watching – perhaps it was Babe Ruth or Legion ball? – but it was clear that the teams were loaded with talent, and that we were seeing a special brand of baseball. As a newcomer to the area, it took me a while to figure out that we had seen a Cape League game, but I realized immediately thereafter that what we had seen was just the tip of an established and wonderful iceberg that hardballers everywhere owe it to themselves to explore.

As much as anything, the Cape Cod Baseball League presents the game at its purest. Sure, there are modern-day professional fingerprints all over it in the form of the scouts that swarm at All Star time, and in the way the major league draft siphons players away from the Cape and into the minors. But the on-field strategies employed are right out of the original Spalding Guide, the players all hustle, and the fans enjoy a level of access that simply no longer exists in the pros, and is rare even in the college ranks.

At the Cape League's Hall of Fame induction ceremony in November 2004, former manager and commissioner Bob Stead noted that "any successful organization has one constant," a unifying thread that links the organization's past to its future. In this observer's view, the Cape League's 'constant' is this remarkable accessibility, for the spirit it produces connects people of all generations, genders, and ethnicities, and creates a sense of community by rallying the towns and the townspeople around their local teams.

This book celebrates this sense of inclusion and belonging, and answers the myriad questions I had following that first Chatham game. Remarkably, the deeper I dug, the better the story got, for no one save a few political party-poopers had any complaints about the way the league operates or what it stands for. In fact, the only real problem I encountered was the need to use the term "head coach" to identify the orchestrator of the team on the field. The Cape League is a college-level circuit and thus uses this college-level expression – but everybody knows that baseball teams are run by "managers," so I am using that word in the places it is required.

Thank you for joining me on my road trip around the Cape. See you at the ballyard!

– Steve Weissman

America's Pastime, New England Style

Wareham players of yore exult as a small boy peers from behind (courtesy Dan Dunn Collectables)

What *is* it About This Game?

There's little question that baseball has deeply entrenched itself in the American collective psyche: credit card commercials celebrating family time are set in baseball stadiums (e.g., MasterCard), movies exploring personal growth and cross-generational relationships frequently use baseball as a backdrop (e.g., *Sandlot, Frequency*), and seaside sand sculpture contests nearly always feature baseball-themed designs. So it is clear that the game has touched us in a way other sports have not.

Part of why this is so undoubtedly has to do with baseball's long history, for whether you believe it was Abner Doubleday, James Cartwright, or Bill James who invented the modern game, its roots run to the early 19th century, a time when our nation itself began coming of age. Many of the immigrants who came to our shores during that period viewed the game as uniquely American, and though they may not have understood it well, they embraced it as a symbol of their new homeland. For many of their children, playing ball was a natural way to join the cultural mainstream, and for the select few talented enough to make a career as a player, it was an effective way to achieve the kind of fame and fortune their parents had come to this country to seek.

Today, baseball is so tightly woven into the fabric of our society that we sometimes don't even know it's there: it's constantly in the background as radio broadcasts waft through open summer windows and water-cooler conversations start the office day. But let something significant happen – a perfect game, a player strike, a major trade – and it's once again front and center both as a current event and a remembrance of things past. ("Remember Seaver's imperfect game against the Cubs in '69? ... the players' strike that cancelled the World Series in '94? ... Kiner, Garagiola, Pollet, and Metkovich for Atwell, Schultz, Ward, Freese, Addis, and Hermanski '53?")

It is this timelessness and sense of shared experience that makes baseball so special, and nowhere are these characteristics more in evidence than they are in the Cape Cod Baseball League. Considered the nation's premier college-level summer league, it has developed a devoted following among players and coaches, scouts and agents, tourists and townspeople, and hundreds of dedicated volunteers who put in thousands of hours of work each year to ensure the games can on.

Each of these groups is attracted by the opportunity to watch young talent and identify the superstars of tomorrow. But the roles that they play and their reasons for involvement vary quite widely, and it is this intersection of expectations – and the fact that everyone goes home satisfied – that gives the Cape League that special character that advertisers, film-makers, sand sculptors, and we all are working so hard to capture.

A New Season Dawns

Here in New England, winter begins much earlier than it does elsewhere, for it is marked not by the moment of solstice, but by the final out of the final game of the Boston Red Sox baseball season.

◊ Some years it comes early, as it did in 1965, when the Sox finished 62-100 and 40 games behind the front-running Minnesota Twins.

◊ Some years it arrives abruptly, as it did in 2003, when they lost a winner-take-all post-season game on a walk-off 11th inning home run by the New York Yankees' Aaron Boone.

◊ Some years it teases, as it did in 1986, when the Sox first faced playoff elimination by the California Angels but rallied to qualify for the World Series, and then needed just one more strike to take the Series from the New York Mets but ended up blowing leads in both Games 6 *and* 7.

◊ And some years – every 86 or so – it ends in unbridled joy, as it did in 2004 following a stunning four-game comeback against the Yankees for the American League championship, and a World Series sweep of the St. Louis Cardinals for all the marbles.

Happily, though, spring arrives much earlier here too. Well before robins appear on suburban front lawns, the Red Sox equipment truck is loaded at Fenway Park and, in an event no less ceremonious than the ground hog's annual appearance in Punxatawney, Pennsylvania, departs for the green fields of Ft. Myers, Florida, where spring training will soon begin.

You may think these comments something of an overstatement, but bear in mind that New England is home to no fewer than 14 professional hardball teams that play in six different leagues that include two independent circuits and major league baseball itself. And as even a casual listener to local sports radio can attest, the individual outcomes of these games are often reviewed and rehashed with no less intensity in the off-season than they were when the games were actually played. So the sport clearly occupies the area's center of attention.

This being the case, it would be logical to conclude that the world of New England baseball has been fairly well explored. But in one corner of the region, one glittering jewel still seems yet to be fully uncovered: this is the Cape Cod Baseball League, which as an amateur organization is unfettered by the public and political pressures that are so integral to professional operations, and can focus wholly on providing a rich experience for fans and players alike.

120 Years of Cape League Baseball

The Cape League officially considers its historical origin to be 1885, a year when Grover Cleveland succeeded Chester Arthur as President of the United States and Cap Anson's Chicago White Stockings captured the National League (yes, *National* League) crown. Unofficially, however, baseball on the Cape dates back to at least 1865, when sea captain Edward Nichols invited a team to play on his field on School Street in Sandwich. Dubbed the Nichols Club in his honor, his is believed to be the first organized team on the Cape and almost certainly included Civil War soldiers who had learned the game on the battlefield and brought it home with them.

The earliest known scorebook from Cape Cod dates from 1867, just seven years after sportswriter Henry Chadwick compiled baseball's first rule book and nine years before the National League – and what we now call Major League Baseball – was born. So there is plenty of tradition to be drawn upon, even if some of the details remain as much accepted account as proven fact. (Did Pie Traynor really play for Falmouth and Mickey Cochrane for Middleboro in the late 'teens and early 'twenties?)

Cape Cod baseball was an amateur, largely town-team, affair even after the first so-named "Cape League" was formed in 1923, and it continued this way all the way to 1963,

Earliest known scorebook, 1867 (courtesy Dan Dunn Collectables)

when it was officially sanctioned by the NCAA as a collegiate circuit and a rule requiring college eligibility was instituted for all players not already on a roster. In 1975, the Cape League began allowing the use of the aluminum bats that colleges by then had adopted to lower their costs.[1] But in 1984, the Cape League decided to switch back to wood, and its standing as a proving ground for potential professionals was instantly and irrevocably enhanced.

Using Wood to Test Players' Mettle

Because aluminum bats have significantly larger "sweet spots" and typically are more evenly balanced than their wooden counterparts, they are much more forgiving should

Sign announcing early Cape rivalry, 1885 (courtesy National Baseball Hall of Fame Library, Cooperstown, NY)

---

[1] Because aluminum bats don't break and wooden ones do, they don't need to be replaced as often and in the long run are much less expensive to use.

a ball be mis-hit, and are somewhat easier to swing with the speed needed to generate long-ball power. The result is something a baseball purist would consider to be a different game than originally intended, one in which higher batting averages, more home runs, and generally higher-scoring games are the norm.

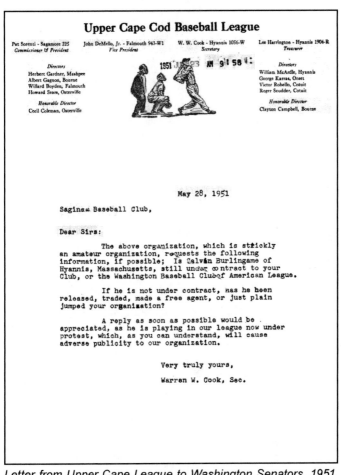

Letter from Upper Cape League to Washington Senators, 1951, confirming the amateur status of Cotuit native and future Cape League Hall of Famer Cal Burlingame (courtesy Dan Dunn Collectables)

Cape Cod Baseball Timeline

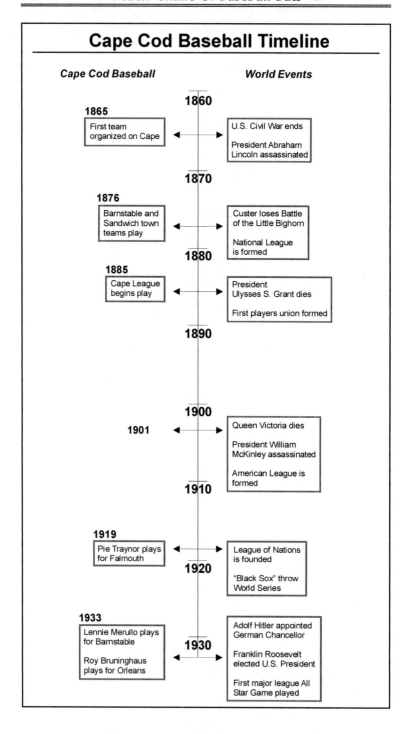

Cape Cod Baseball   **World Events**

1860

1865
First team
organized on Cape   ◄────►   U.S. Civil War ends

President Abraham
Lincoln assassinated

1870

1876
Barnstable and
Sandwich town   ◄────►   Custer loses Battle
teams play   of the Little Bighorn

National League
1880   is formed

1885
Cape League
begins play   ◄────►   President
Ulysses S. Grant dies

First players union formed

1890

1900

1901   ◄────►   Queen Victoria dies

President William
McKinley assassinated

American League is
1910   formed

1919
Pie Traynor plays
for Falmouth   ◄────►   League of Nations
1920   is founded

"Black Sox" throw
World Series

1933
Lennie Merullo plays   Adolf Hitler appointed
for Barnstable   German Chancellor
1930
Roy Bruninghaus   ◄────►   Franklin Roosevelt
plays for Orleans   elected U.S. President

First major league All
Star Game played

Cape Cod Baseball Timeline

Cape Cod Baseball

World Events

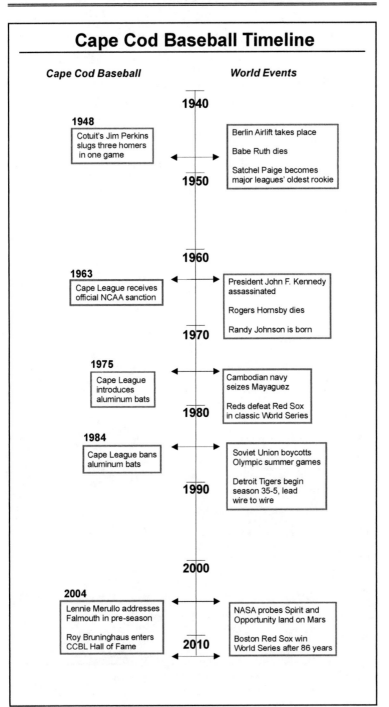

1940

1948
Cotuit's Jim Perkins slugs three homers in one game

Berlin Airlift takes place

Babe Ruth dies

Satchel Paige becomes major leagues' oldest rookie

1950

1960

1963
Cape League receives official NCAA sanction

President John F. Kennedy assassinated

Rogers Hornsby dies

Randy Johnson is born

1970

1975
Cape League introduces aluminum bats

Cambodian navy seizes Mayaguez

Reds defeat Red Sox in classic World Series

1980

1984
Cape League bans aluminum bats

Soviet Union boycotts Olympic summer games

Detroit Tigers begin season 35-5, lead wire to wire

1990

2000

2004
Lennie Merullo addresses Falmouth in pre-season

Roy Bruninghaus enters CCBL Hall of Fame

NASA probes Spirit and Opportunity land on Mars

Boston Red Sox win World Series after 86 years

2010

As a result, scouts, agents, and other talent evaluators have a more difficult time projecting the potential of a player using an aluminum bat – or a pitcher facing one – than one using wood.

Taking the metal out of the equation therefore better simulates professional game conditions, and allows observers of all stripes – including casual fans – to more accurately gauge how well a player might perform as he moves up the skills ladder. So when the Cape League returned to the use of wood, it immediately emerged as the country's preeminent college summer league, and it began to attract the widespread following it enjoys today.

For the players, the Cape League provides the first true test of their baseball skills and stamina. Daily high-caliber competition, extended separation from friends and family, and uncomfortable bus rides to and from games are part of

The more things change: Falmouth fans enjoy a game in 1914 ...
(courtesy Dan Dunn collectables)

the package both on the Cape and in the minors; how well they hold up here therefore may shed light on how well they may fare at the next level. Knowing this, big-league scouts and agents patrol the premises to get a jump-start on their own responsibilities, which boil down to discovering and contracting players with the highest potential ceiling.

For the fans, the Cape League provides a window into the future of the sport by showcasing young talent and challenging observers to identify the big league stars of three and four years hence. It also serves as great family entertainment, for the players are clean-cut and kid-friendly, the on-field play is spirited, and the opportunity to simply *have fun* is unparalleled. And since there is no set admission fee (though donations are encouraged and gladly accepted), it is hard to beat in terms of overall value.

... and in 2004.

For the locals, the League serves as a rallying point in a way that may surprise those who think of it as a more transient experience. Sure, the players turn over every year or two as their college eligibility expires and/or they enter the professional ranks. And sure, many in the crowd are tourists who may or may not return later in their vacations or perhaps next year. But for the year-round residents and full-time "summer people" who call the Cape their home, the local teams are a source of civic pride, and the local townspeople turn out by the thousands to root their boys to victory.

At the end of the day, the Cape Cod Baseball League turns out to be much more of a community than an athletic association, for it is a central point at which all manner of individuals gather to share an experience. The players, their families, and their host families; the team coaches, executives, and game-day volunteers; the reporters who cover the games and the professionals who track the players' progress; the umpires and the fans ... they come from many different places and for many different reasons, but come they do, and with the same essential purpose in mind: to revel in a powerful sense of promise and possibility that will nourish them during the short summer season and sustain them during the long, dark winter. For as sure as Sox fans look forward to the departure of the team's equipment truck, so does the Cape League community anticipate the renewal of their special bond, and the chance to extend the continuum of tradition that began so long ago.

The Cape League's Fields of Dreams

Light towers glow on a lazy summer night in Falmouth.

Ballyards by the Sea

Cape Cod Baseball League games are played at ball fields that are as welcoming as any you might imagine. Some evoke a *Field of Dreams*-style mysticism, others are as accessible as the neighborhood playgrounds they practically are, but all are well-described by Cape Cod Times intern D.C. Reeves, who says, "If you can walk from one gate to the other without going around the backstop, you're probably at a Cape League game."

The intimacy of the fields often comes as something of a surprise to players who are new to the league, for the sophistication and dimensions of the facilities here are somewhat different than they may be used to. Because many of the players come from large schools with major baseball programs, they are accustomed to playing in stadium-like structures with full-time groundskeepers. Thanks in large part to the Cape League's high visibility and stellar reputation, they therefore expect to find much of the same when they get here, but they discover something quite different the instant as they arrive.

"The lighting at some of the fields is tough," says Falmouth Commodore Paul Christian. "Then throw in some school's ace throwing 98 [mph], and a little fog," and the dimension of the players' new challenge becomes clear. Still, most come to like the informality of their new surroundings, and Hyannis Met Mike Costanzo sums up the general reaction well. "I thought the fields would be better groomed and more like stadiums," he says. "But I like [what I found] because I like old-school baseball."

Less attractive – especially among pitchers – is the general uncertainty surrounding the actual depth of the outfield fences around the league, for it is fairly universally acknowledged that many of the distance-from-home-plate markers are better characterized as rough guidelines than true measurements.

As this season progresses, much of the griping centers on the new fences in Falmouth, which appear to be considerably closer to the plate than advertised. Brewster righthander Scott Lonergan remembers a Commodore hitting an easy fly ball for a home run, "and even he laughed as he rounded first." At one point, someone seeks to put the discussion to rest by chalking a new figure on the sign in center field, but the original is soon restored, and pitchers again lament what they see as an unfair hitter's advantage.

The Orleans Cardinals occupy the rustic visitor's dugout in Brewster.

Falmouth general manager Chuck Sturtevant admits that new, shorter fences were indeed installed in one half of the outfield prior to the season and that the old signs were merely rehung without being corrected. But he also notes an interesting psychology is at work, for most of the home runs being hit in Falmouth are leaving the yard via the opposite power alley, and that dimension did *not* change. "Isn't it funny," says one observer, "how it is the number painted on the fence that is the problem, and not the pitchers' inability to keep the ball down!"

Bourne Braves

Coady School Field, with the landmark Bourne Bridge in the background

The Bourne Braves play at Coady School Field, practically in the shadow of one of the two bridges that span the Cape Cod Canal. Located at the intersection of two neighborhood streets, the field sits amidst the daily lives of those who reside nearby, and is as natural a part of their families as their children and their aunts. However, it is oriented in a way that causes the setting sun to shine directly into the batters' eyes, requiring that games on sunny days be halted for 15 minutes or so until the glare disappears. A new field is currently being built and should be ready in 2006, at which time this oddity will cease to be an issue.

Brewster Whitecaps

Cape Cod Tech Field from atop the famous hill

The Brewster Whitecaps also play in a schoolyard, except theirs sits behind Cape Cod Tech, a regional technical high school just over the line in Harwich whose horticulture students use the field as a practical laboratory. Team volunteers believe their field affords fans the best view of a game that can be found anywhere, a function of the 30-foot hill that lines the right side of the diamond, atop which people perch their beach chairs or settle into a small set of bleachers. Like the Braves, the Whitecaps are slated to move to a new field in 2006, this one in the town of Brewster itself and equipped with the lights that are missing from their current quarters.

Chatham A's

Veteran's Field, Chatham

Chatham's Veteran's Field may be one of the better known Cape League ballyards because of the exposure it received in the 2001 film *Summer Catch* and the 2004 book *The Last Best League*, both of which focused on the hometown Athletics. Set back from the main street of Route 28, it is walking distance from the chic downtown, and its natural bowl shape imbues it with some of the best overall sightlines anywhere. The field also has lights, which means games can be played well into the night – unless the cool air blowing off the nearby ocean spawns the heavy fog Chatham fans know so well.

Cotuit Kettleers

Lowell Park, Cotuit

Cotuit's Lowell Park is carved out of the woods in the same way the Field of Dreams was cut from a cornfield. Home to the Kettleers, it is tucked deep within a leafy neighborhood and blends in so well with its surroundings that it can easily be missed when driving by. Tint a photo of the field with sepia tones and, but for the light towers, it would be easy to believe the field has been there since the very first Cape League pitch was thrown.

Falmouth Commodores

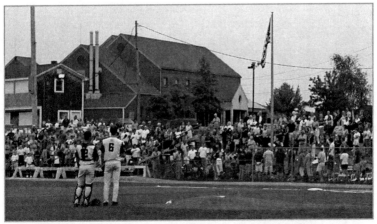

Guv Fuller Field, Falmouth as the national anthem is played

The Falmouth Commodores play at Guv Fuller Field on the Arnie Allen Diamond, which is named after a beloved 40-year team volunteer who succumbed to cancer in late 2003. Located behind the police station and a community center on the main drag of Route 28, it is a lighted facility that sits astride the ordinary comings and goings of summer life and unfolds behind the parking lot like a carpet of fun. It may be best known among players and baseball professionals for its old temporary outfield fence, which prior to its recent reinforcement had been known to "swallow" unsuspecting fielders.

Harwich Mariners

Whitehouse Field, Harwich, as the fog descends

Harwich's Whitehouse Field, home to the Mariners, sits amidst a typical Cape neighborhood at the end of a long driveway and large parking lot that also serve adjacent school buildings. Surrounded by trees and featuring lights, it possesses the most complete scoreboard in the league, including not only a full nine-inning line score but also the ability to display the batter's name, number, and game performance.

Hyannis Mets

McKeon Park, Hyannis, from atop the broadcast roof (courtesy Bill Bussiere)

The Hyannis Mets are at home at McKeon Park, which is located behind a church and a closed-up high school. A long fly ball from the harbor in one direction and the trendy downtown in the other, it may be best known for the ospreys that attend each game: according to legend, families of birds roosted atop the illumination towers that once ringed the field, and as a result, only day games could be played lest the hot lights disturb the nests. The less-romantic truth is that the towers had fallen into disrepair and could not be used, and though a recent refurbishment has since taken the towers down, the ospreys remain and can be seen swooping and soaring over the game below.

Orleans Cardinals

Eldredge Park, Orleans during the home run derby at the All Star game

The Orleans Cardinals play at Eldredge Park, a lighted field that is rimmed on two sides by intersecting major streets and sits below the Nauset Middle School on a third. Fans in attendance feel as if they've been transported into a post card of baseball on the Cape, not in the least because of the presence of Mr. Cardinal, a private citizen and team committee member who doubles as the team's unofficial mascot.

Wareham Gatemen

Clem Spillane Field, Wareham as pre-game practice begins

Clem Spillane Field, home to the Wareham Gatemen, is built into the hill behind Wareham Town Hall. The only field on the north side of the Cape Cod Canal, it is especially notable for its stone-dust infield and a left-field bullpen that sits 10 feet above the outfield grass. It also features lights and has an extensive set of bleachers, so if there is one place to which it may not be necessary to bring a beach chair, this is it.

Yarmouth-Dennis Red Sox

Red Wilson Field, Yarmouth hosts a playoff crowd

The Yarmouth-Dennis Red Sox play at Red Wilson Field in a sprawling athletic complex behind Dennis-Yarmouth Regional High School. Unpretentious and accessible, the central diamond plays host to the Cape League collegians even as the outlying soccer, lacrosse, and baseball fields give grade-schoolers and their friends a place to run around. The effect is one of relaxed family fun and is what all visitors to the Cape League have come to find.

The Tie That Binds

Regardless of where they play, the athletes who grace these fields recognize that their time on the Cape grants them membership in a very exclusive club, and it turns out that the connection they share carries forward even into the major leagues.

Former Brewster Whitecap and San Diego Padre Dave Staton remembers the first time he went into San Francisco as a major leaguer, partly because it was his first opportunity to play first base in front of a "horde of friends and family," and partly because of a special encounter he had with Giants slugger and ex-Kettleer Will Clark. "I had a really good series against the Giants, who were in a pennant race against the Atlanta Braves at the time," he recalls. A Clark single brought the two into close contact for the first time, which thrilled Staton because Clark had been one of his heroes as a high schooler just a few years before.

"He leaned over and said, 'Hey, man, way to swing the bat!'" Staton recalls. "It really touched me when he said that because being a rookie in the big leagues, you are basically at the bottom of the pole. So for him to acknowledge that I was swinging the bat well just led to an unbelievable feeling." For Clark, the recognition was merely natural. "I said something to Dave because we had something in common," he says on the day he and Staton were inducted into the Cape League Hall of Fame. "Not only were we ballplayers on the Cape, but we went on to professional ball, and it seemed like we kept bumping into one another."

Former Falmouth Commodore and current Cincinnati Red Eric Milton tells a similar tale. "You talk about it with every team you play against," he says. "I'll say, 'Hey I played against you on the Cape!' and the guy will say 'Yeah, you did.'"

Milton was a Falmouth teammate of current Los Angeles Angel of Anaheim Adam Kennedy, and when the two squared off during Milton's time with the Minnesota Twins, "we would talk about our time down the Cape." Milton, by the way, is the only player to pitch a no-hitter both on the Cape and in the major leagues, and not only did he victimize Kennedy's Angels in his big-league no-no, but his catcher in that game was former Cotuit Kettleer Terry Steinbach. So the connections are pervasive, and they run quite deep even when a player doesn't go on to the majors.

Eric Milton as a Falmouth Commodore (courtesy Dan Dunn Collectables)

The Dream on Display: the Cape League Hall of Fame

Nowhere is this more evident than during the annual Hall of Fame induction ceremony, which recognizes a select few individuals who have brought something exceptional to the Cape League in terms of either on-field performance or off-field participation. Held about 10 weeks after the season ends, it reaches back through time to honor those whose contributions have made the league what it is today and connect them with those who are carrying the tradition forward now.

The Hall of Fame itself is located at the Heritage Museum and Gardens in Sandwich, Massachusetts, and features a per-

The Cape Cod Baseball League Hall of Fame at Heritage Museum and Gardens, Sandwich

manent display of historic photographs, personal effects, and team memorabilia. It also includes the special plaques that salute the players, organizers, officials, and others who have been inducted thus far. Fans wishing to gain a measure of what the league is about surely should put it on their list of sites to see.

Off-Season Moves and Grooves

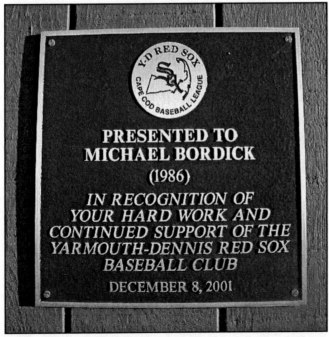

Plaque commemorating the contributions of former Y-D star and long-time major leaguer Mike Bordick in support of Red Sox operations

Pre-Season's Greetings

The Cape League's pre-season begins immediately upon the close of the season before, as the managers and general managers huddle to discuss their player options for the following summer, and their resources for recruiting athletes who not only can perform inside the lines, but behave like gentlemen outside them. At the same time, the league elects its officers, approves its operating budget, establishes the next year's playing schedule, and debates many other important items.

The teams themselves hold regular internal meetings to debate and address issues relating to such diverse activities as concessions, merchandising, field improvement, player and host family recruitment, local corporate sponsorships, the procurement of uniforms and equipment, and general fund raising – in short, absolutely *everything* that goes into maximizing the game experience both on the field and off.

In typical New England fashion, each team operates independently of the others, and of the league itself – even when some cooperation might make financial sense. One oft-told tale involves the opportunity for the franchises to enjoy a significant discount on team caps if all 10 clubs agreed to buy them from the same manufacturer – only to have the deal disintegrate when one team refuses to go along because it means severing the relationship it has had with a local provider for the better part of a decade. Taken together, the league and the teams – non-profit organizations all, and staffed nearly exclusively by volunteers – manage about $1.8 million worth of budget, so the decisions they make are not insignificant in the aggregate.

This right of self-determination is part of what makes the Cape League so intriguing, for the circuit's very existence depends upon its ability to achieve consensus on many core

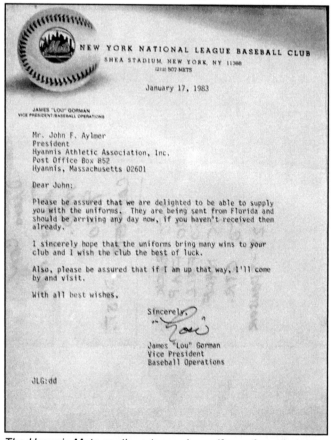

The Hyannis Mets continue to receive uniforms from their New York namesake and annually seal the deal with a few Cape Cod lobsters (courtesy Hyannis Mets)

issues. Some of these are relatively straightforward, such as setting universal minimum standards for the players' Code of Conduct and increasing the number of players that can be signed prior to the season from 23 to 25, two initiatives enacted before the 2005 season. But others are more contentious, such as the proposal prior to 2004 that buses be hired to transport every team's players to and from road games, rather than allow them to drive themselves.

This measure ultimately was passed and put to rest growing concerns about safety and liability. But before it was, a spirited debate took place about the budget ramifications of the move – not so much because of the need to pay for the buses and the drivers, an expense that would be covered by special league-level sponsorships, but because of the need for the teams to feed the players *en route* since they'd no longer have the opportunity to grab a fast-food bite on their way to the field.

Much of the credit for seeing that any differences of team opinion are reconciled quickly and fruitfully goes to Cape League president Judy Walden Scarafile, who is a master of meeting management and great facilitator of organizational collaboration. Utilizing Robert's Rules of Order in a way that would thrill the general who created them, she is able to keep the league's proceedings moving despite the large number of committee reports and new initiatives that make up any given agenda. It is also an enormous help that the dozens of people in the room – and the scores of volunteers they represent – are all there for the same single reason: to create a high-quality summer baseball experience for everyone who is touched by the game.

Thus it is after a particularly discordant series of meetings regarding league voting rights, commissioner Paul Galop moves that the issue be tabled until after the season, saying simply "let's play baseball." The motion is met with universal agreement and a general sense of relief, and it passes in a rush of unanimity that lacks only a series of "huzzahs" from the other delegates to complete the image of a parliamentary body at work.

Setting the Schedule: Who Plays When, and Where

Putting the schedule together is a surprisingly difficult task that involves far more than ensuring that five games are played every day. For one thing, not every field has lights, so the games planned for the ones without must start early enough to ensure they can be completed before the sun goes down. But they can't be scheduled for *too* early in the day because the volunteers staffing the souvenir stores, working concession stands, and passing the hat all have day jobs and are not free to come to the field until quitting time.

Another consideration is the need to schedule the same number of weekend home games for each team. Vacation rentals on the Cape typically run Saturday to Saturday, so each weekend brings a new wave of tourists to the area who may be looking for something predictable, easy, and fun to do on their first day in town. Also, most local folk do not have to work on the weekend and may be more likely to take in a game than during the week. So the net effect is that the weekend crowds tend to be larger than their weekday counterparts, and the teams' gate, merchandise, and food receipts tend to be higher accordingly. As a result, the teams all covet Saturday and Sunday home dates.

Adding to the schedule-maker's fun is the need to include several open dates that can be used to play games postponed because of rain. This is harder than it sounds, though, for the season is very short and already includes two immovable interruptions: one about two-thirds of the way through for the All Star game, and the other at the very end for playoff "play-in" games should teams finish in a tie for a post-season berth. So finding additional days throughout the summer to accommodate bad weather is no easy task.

Yet another factor is at least as equally important as all the others, and is the subject of an interesting push-pull that lies at the heart of many Cape League issues: namely, balancing the needs and desires of the Cape League and its franchises with those of major league baseball, which is a major contributor to the Cape League cause.

For the most part, these two perspectives are perfectly synchronized, as both want to see that as many games are played as possible in the limited time available. But the devil is in the details, and so the League's scheduling committee tries to stagger the starting times so the scouts can attend more than one game in a day.

This dynamic sometimes extends to non-game issues as well, as is the case this particular autumn when the festivities surrounding the league's annual All Star game threatens to overlap with a player showcase being held in North Carolina. Unless the schedule can be adjusted, most of the scouts on the Cape for the All Star game will have to leave immediately after the last out is made in order to make the showcase on time. Since part of what scouts appreciate most about their Cape League experience is the ability to mingle with current and potential draftees, the league votes to recast its All Star agenda so the scouts will have more time to complete their appointed rounds, and the players still will have their moment in the sun.

Building the Rosters: Who Plays, and For Whom

Putting a team together can be equally challenging, as it requires managers and general managers to juggle NCAA rules, player capabilities, and team chemistry in their pursuit of a championship.

To take part in the Cape League, players must be invited to join a team, and they actually sign a contract in much the same way they commit to a college program. In addition, they must have NCAA eligibility remaining at the start of the Cape League season, a requirement that means neither high schoolers nor college seniors qualify to play. In a year the basketball draft featured numerous 12th-grade picks, one cynical fan was thus moved to remark, "This league is more strict than the NBA!"

The Cape League itself does not recruit players; instead, each team builds its own roster, usually by leveraging a network of contacts that has been constructed over the years by the manager and general manager. (A few players also do emerge from an invitation-only tryout held just prior to the season.) Because the League is highly competitive – amateur status having nothing to do with the desire to win – situations occasionally do arise in which several teams may vie for the same player's services. In such cases, the outcome is generally determined by the tenor of the relationship that is developing between the player and his prospective manager, the extent of the player's familiarity with his potential teammates, and perhaps the character of his prospective home town.

Only Good Guys Need Apply

In deciding whom to invite, teams look not only at a player's baseball skills, but at his strength of character as well. "I'll call a college coach and ask, 'what kind of kid is he?'" says Yarmouth-Dennis Red Sox manager Scott Pickler, who like his colleagues around the league knows that the season is too intense, the quarters too close, and the responsibility to the host families too great to allow for any nonsense.

Underscoring how seriously this issue is taken, the teams all have formal handbooks that contain a Code of Conduct to which their players must adhere or risk being asked to leave.

Brewster Whitecaps host parent Annie Blatz reports, "I've been pleasantly surprised with how well-mannered my players all have been," and it is clear from the way players are vetted that this is no accident.

Khalil Greene letter of commitment, 2000 (courtesy Falmouth Commodores)

Ann Sullivan remembers well the initial trepidation and ultimate joy she felt when she first became a house parent. "In 1988, my husband and I became a host family for the Whitecaps," she recalls. "It was the Whitecaps' first year, and David [Staton] was our first player. At 6' 5" and 200 pounds, he entered our small ranch house, and we wondered whether we'd have our hands full. But it turned out that David was a wonderful person and a great baseball player," and in the end, their summer together was special for them both – so special, in fact, that 16 years later, he asked her to present him for induction into the Cape League Hall of Fame.

Tending the Revolving Door

Even after they're set, rosters on the Cape constantly turn over due to the signing of pro contracts, family situations, and injuries suffered both before and during the Cape League season. In addition, the chance to try out for Team USA or other nations' Olympic squads also siphons talent away from the Cape, and NCAA rules further limit the number of college teammates that can be on the same summer team, and prohibit a player from playing for his own college coach. The idea here is to keep the summer season from becoming an extension of the regular college season, and the ultimate irony is that Cape League managers are therefore unable to sign the very players they know best.

To help ensure at least some continuity, teams can protect lower-classmen they wish to have return, and thereby keep their competitors from luring their top talent away with promises of more playing time, fancier living quarters, or other NCAA-acceptable inducements. Individual strategies are also employed to mitigate the effect of player churn. For example, Y-D decided three years ago to concentrate more on recruiting sophomores than it had in the past, figuring that since they are not subject to draft, they may be more likely to commit quickly to the team and to stay for the entire season. At the same time, the team also decided to spend more time seeking players from New England both to boost the local interest and to minimize the cost of sending players home, which all the teams cover. (They are not required to cover the cost of coming to the Cape, however, though many times they do.)

If all this doesn't make a manager's and general manager's jobs hard enough, then also consider the fact that many recruits are still competing in the College World Series when the Cape League season begins – they are, after all, the cream of the college baseball crop, so it stands to reason that their teams would go deep into their post-season. To field a full team, therefore, most teams must begin their year with temporary players on hand, and it may be weeks before the originally-intended squad actually takes the field.

Temporary and Replacement Players

Temporary players are critical to every Cape League team because their performance can dictate how many wins their team can accumulate at the season's start, and thereby how likely the team is to make the playoffs at the summer's end. Solid performers can and do make the roster as permanent players – Brewster's Will Rhymes and Falmouth's Paul Christian are two such examples this year – but they all know that even a brief time on the Cape is hugely valuable, personally validating, and a whole lot of fun besides.

During the season, especially as the playoffs loom, teams look at the players they have, those they've lost to injuries or family situations, and others with skills or attitudes that may be useful down the stretch, and they reengineer their squads accordingly. Players must be on the roster on July 31 to take part in the post-season, so many of the names, faces, and uniform numbers change suddenly as of that date.

The challenge is to find some who not only are good enough for the Cape, but who aren't already playing in another college summer league. This can take a bit of looking, and often comes down to timing, since a number of the other leagues wrap up before the Cape League does.

Ramon Glasgow, a late-season addition to the Y-D Red Sox this year, hardly knew where Cape Cod is when his college coach called to ask if he'd be interested in playing with the team, but he is happy to be here, barely 48 hours after getting the word. "I've never been around such great players," he says, and his joy and wonder are apparent for all to see. About the only fly in the ointment was the cost of the plane ticket needed to bring Glasgow from his California home, an expense Y-D decided to cover to speed Glasgow on his way. Thus, GM Jim Martin is prompted to kid Pickler, "What's the matter; you couldn't find anyone east of the Mississippi?"

Player Profile: Will Rhymes

Brewster second baseman Will Rhymes is having the time of his life. A pre-med major at William and Mary, he has been playing baseball and only baseball since he was six years old, and was a shortstop until he reached high school and found his way blocked by a "stud" player already at the position. "So I switched to second," he says, and he had little problem with the change because "I'm a small guy, but quick."

Rhymes wanted to attend college outside of Texas, and "the only scholarship offer I received was from William and Mary." That decision thus easily made, he entered school with doctoring on his mind. But like so many students, he rethought this decision shortly thereafter, and more recently, he rethought it again. As a result, "my schedule is now stacked with courses so I can catch up with the program," he says.

This spring, he received a call from his college coach, who wanted to know if he was interested in playing on the Cape. This decision was as easy as choosing his college. "I was ecstatic!" Rhymes enthuses, even after learning that he'd be joining the Whitecaps as a temporary player.

Brewster is not the most thickly settled of communities, and Rhymes is struck by the lack of commercialization he finds when he arrives there. "You have to drive 20 minutes just to find fast food!" he exclaims, and he is enjoying to the utmost what he describes as being a "pure" experience.

The best part, he says, is that after years of dreaming about it and working for it, "I'm living the life." At a school like William and Mary, "the fact that I play baseball is kind of unimportant. Here, though, I'm a ballplayer, and that's all."

Immediately upon donning a uniform, Rhymes sets about making the most of his abilities, and not only plays his way onto the permanent roster, but is named to the All Star squad as well. All this success is leaving him feeling a bit overwhelmed, and more than just a little torn between the two lives that he may soon need to choose between. On the other hand, he points out, "You can always go back and be a doctor, but you can't go back to be a ballplayer." So he finishes the season tied for fourth in the league with a .308 batting average and leading his team in stolen bases, and he returns to school knowing these twin facts may yet help turn his dream into reality.

Chatham A's manager John Schiffner had no such problem in 2002, when his pitching staff was decimated by injuries, a parent's serious medical condition forced one of his hurlers to immediately fly home, and a surprise contract signing took another off the eligible list on the very day he was scheduled to pitch. Down to only eight arms, he recalls, "I gathered everybody in the dugout and said, 'I need some help. Does anybody know anyone from their college who's not in an NCAA summer league and can get here real fast? Greg Conden from George Washington University raised his hand and said, 'Coach, my roommate's available.' I said, 'Great! Here's my cell phone – call him!' And he said, 'I don't have to; he's right there!' The kid was sitting in the bleachers, and we signed him on the spot." For Dennis Gramolini, it was an express ticket to the Cape League, and "considering the circumstances," Schiffner says, "it was like getting Randy Johnson."

For the players coming in, the opportunity to play in the Cape League is seen as a windfall, even as it may feel awkward to parachute into an established team. Andrew Larsen, for example, is finding it difficult to fit into the Bourne Braves as the replacement for the team's injured center fielder, not in the least because he attends the State University of New York at Stony Brook and not one of the large "baseball factories" that provide so much of the Cape League's talent. But as he points out, there's nothing like contributing in a game situation to smooth the way. "I threw a runner out at home the other day, and that helped a lot!" he says, and he's proving daily to his teammates and to himself just how much he belongs.

In the end, the Cape League finds itself populated by players who possess essentially the same sets of skills and experience, and teams have virtually no opportunity to blend younger players in with veterans so they can slowly learn the ropes. Building for the future thus is not an option the way it is in the major leagues or even at a four-year college; Cape League players are simply dropped onto their fields with the expectation they'll win. "There's so much talent *not* in the Cape League," Bourne general manager Mike Carrier says, that finding good players actually isn't that hard. But finding those who can adjust to place, competition, and team can be difficult and varies every single season. Oddly enough, this is also good news of sorts because it means any given team in any given year has an excellent chance of winning, and there is a certain sense of parity to be found here by the sea.

No Rest for the Weary

Poetic though the Cape League can be, the fact is that putting the season together requires a ton of hard work. Scores of tireless volunteers labor all winter long to put the game on the field, the players in their houses, and the food and merchandise on the shelves, and the fact that it all runs so smoothly is testament to their dedication and effectiveness. Spending time with these people brings new meaning to the phrase "for the love of the game," for the small budgets they have to work with allow for no other meaningful form of compensation.

Bourne's Carrier says the volunteers "are the unsung heroes of the league," and former players look back with affection and awe on the commitment the local folk make to their teams. One-time Cotuit catcher and manager Jack McCarthy remembers well the woman who sang the national anthem before every home game, as well as town postmistress Louise Harman, who brought the players' mail right to the practice field. "She obviously cared about us," McCarthy said. "But as a player, I didn't get it. I understood Arnold [Mycock] was the general manager and took care of a lot of things — we used to kid that he wore so many hats that we'd have to buy him one with all of his jobs printed on it. But why are all these other people doing this?"

McCarthy remembers going to the field in the early afternoons and seeing a bunch of guys smoothing the infield with big wooden rakes. "We didn't have a drag in the '60s," he recalls, "and I used to wonder, as a 19 year old, 'why are they doing this?' I worked at the cemetery, and my boss there worked five and a half days a week — why would he then go to the park and rake the field?"

Most of the time, the reasons involve an eclectic mix of civic pride, childhood dreams, and a desire to give something back to the community. For many, the reasons are so compelling that the line is quickly crossed from merely helping out to becoming a full-fledged volunteer and, often, serving on the team's executive committee. But for all, it is clear that the time they give to a Cape League team is a true labor of love, and they wouldn't have it any other way.

Hosts with the Most

One of the most pressing jobs of the off-season is ensuring every player joining a team has a place to live. It has been well chronicled how local families open their homes to athletes from around the country, but the process of making this happen is something of a wonder.

Perhaps the easiest part involves contacting the host families from the year before to gauge their interest in hosting a player again, for the answer often is a routine "yes" – remarkably, tenures of five, 10, and even 20 years are not uncommon around the league, and most of the long-timers can't believe they've been doing it for the time they have.

Not everyone returns to the fold, of course, as families move or their circumstances change. So the next challenge is to find new homes to replace the departed, or even simply to reduce the load on families that are hosting more than one player.

The actual placing of the players is an art form unto itself as housing coordinators balance personalities, lifestyles, and even geography – for instance, players without cars are housed with or near to players with cars whenever possible so they can more easily get to and from the field. What typically isn't done is to accede to specific requests to house only players of certain positions (pitchers, shortstops, etc.) or from certain schools (Notre Dame is a popular preference), for the rosters change enough during the season to quickly make this unworkable.

In addition, offers to house players are declined when families view the incoming player as a built-in coach for their ballplaying children; in these cases, disappointment and resentment can only ensue because the players are coming specifically to play ball, and that is, and has to be, their first priority. So while pointers usually can be provided during the course of the summer, setting it up to be more than that isn't fair and can only lead to problems.

Having said this, though, meaningful relationships do quickly form between most players and their host families, and "big brother" / "son we never had" kinds of ties usually do end up developing. Sherri Merchant, a first-year host parent in Wareham who originally was asked only to advertise her women's fitness center in the team's yearbook, notes with

Wareham host family members Travis, Sherri, and Bill Merchant

interest and amusement the evolution that occurred between her family and her player. Travis Tully, a Gatemen outfielder from the University of Houston, at first was so dedicated to his craft that he didn't make much time to spend with the Merchants, but he slowly became a fixture at the family table. A month into the season, she writes:

> It was a players' "free day," so I made Mr. Travis (as I affection-ately call [him]) feel 'guilty' (that's what he says to me regularly with his southern accent) and spend the day with us. We actually had a great day [whale watching and going out to dinner] and really got to spend some quality time with him … As corny as this sounds, going to the games has brought our immediate family a sense of unity and structure. We are so busy, but we seem to all rush to get to Mr. Travis' games … Today, Mr. Travis took [my son] Travis with some of the players to hit some golf balls and to dinner! Oh, now tell me my 14-year-old isn't feeling a wee-bit macho and "kewl." Can't wait to finish my 17-hour day and go home to hear the excitement Travis will try to conceal when he tells tales of his day with Mr. Tully and crew!"

The host family plays a critical role in the success of the Cape League, for it serves as the "glue" that binds the player, his own family, and the team. An unhappy placement can have a dire effect on a player's on-field performance and cause heart-ache for the folks at home, who want only for their son to grow both as a player and as a person.

Fortunately, the vast majority of placements work out extremely well, and the relationships that form in a great many instances are life-long. Players commonly invite their host families to attend their weddings, and those that make the big leagues regularly leave tickets at the Will Call window at Fenway Park when their teams come to Boston.

In a wonderful bit of symmetry, the players frequently have just as big an impact on their hosts as well. Paul McCracken, a first-year host father in South Yarmouth, sees the hand of "divine providence" in his decision to house Y-D Red Sox pitcher Brett Harker. "I lost my Dad at the end of May and spent two weeks in Pennsylvania helping my Mom," he relates. "Two days after returning home, Brett showed up. He is an outstanding young man, and he helped me make the transition during a difficult time."

Where the Home Fires Burn

If the players' hosts find their lives enriched by their Cape League experience, then imagine the effect on the players' families! For most, it involves a mix of excitement, nervousness, and separation anxiety, for besides giving their

Y-D pitcher Brett Harker with host parent Paul McCracken (courtesy Paul McCracken)

boys the chance to play ball at a high level, the league also forces them to grow up just a bit. "You're not at home, and Mom or your girlfriend aren't cooking for you, cleaning for you, or doing your laundry," says Ex-Harwich Mariner and former major league star Cory Snyder. "You have to do it all yourself now, and that's a big thing."

This cuts both ways as parents find they must watch from afar as their children pursue their dreams. Sometimes they have a harder time letting go than their sons do, and it is not unusual to hear about a player whose dad has come to the Cape and is now criticizing his son's every move as he struggles to perform at this new, advanced level. This added pressure only makes the task more difficult, and it is fortunate that these instances are more the exceptions than the rule.

It is a major help to both parent and child that the host families are generally so caring and communicative. Karen Curreri, mother of Y-D catcher Frank, says the experience "is everything they promised it would be and more – not only for the players, but for the parents as well." Karen LaMotta, mother of Harwich Mariner Ryan, seems even relieved when says how impressed she is with the depth of community support her son is receiving. "The host family fusses over him, sets rules for him, and encourages him," she notes with evident joy. "We live 2000 miles away, and it's nice to know that somebody cares about our son."

Most families are at least vaguely familiar with the feeling because at this point in their lives, the majority of their sons have already spent years playing on All Star and travel teams. But for many, this may be the first time they are away from home for an extended period, and for nearly all, the baseball stakes have never been higher.

Connecticut-born Ben Crabtree, a catcher with Y-D, has been through the "away" process before thanks to time he spent during high school in a league on Long Island and his stint last year on the Cape with Brewster. This year, his mother Vicki says, "we told him not to worry about us, and just to take care of what he needs to do." As it turns out, she and her husband Art are spending a lot of time here anyway, but it still isn't easy, and parents the league over all appreciate the lengths to which the host families and league officials go to welcome and support their children.

Y-D Red Sox players honor and thank their host families in a special on-field ceremony that is conducted, in some fashion, by all 10 teams.

Player Profile: Ben Crabtree

Ben Crabtree and two of his legions of young fans

Ben Crabtree is from Roxberry, Connecticut and is heading into his senior year at Ohio University, where he is studying organizational communications. He played in Brewster last season and is enjoying his second summer on the Cape as a catcher for the Y-D Red Sox.

As a youth, Crabtree could be found both on the hill and behind the plate, and he chose catching over pitching when entered high school because "I figured it would be easier to switch back to pitching if I needed to than to go from pitcher back to catcher." After a summer playing ball on Long Island and a year of prep school, he participated in a baseball showcase and attracted particular interest from Old Dominion and Ohio University. Ohio got the nod because he instantly liked the campus and thought he'd have a good chance to make the team as a freshman. Later, with two successful college seasons under his belt, Crabtree found himself playing for the Brewster Whitecaps and enjoying the experience to the fullest. But in a college game this past the spring, "I called for a curve, and got a fastball," and the result was a wrist injury that not only cost him much of the rest of his season, but the chance to be drafted as well.

"I believe everything happens for a reason," he says, "and though I was angry for the first few days, I learned a lot from my injury." To keep in shape, he studied effective conditioning techniques and proper nutrition. But perhaps the most important knowledge he gained is just how important his sport is to him even if he doesn't end up playing professionally. Whatever happens next, Crabtree declares, "baseball definitely will be a part of my life." The dream still burns fiercely within him, of course, but he can see himself as a college coach, for he'd like to share his experiences with future up-and-comers the way his coaches shared theirs with him. Meanwhile, he is thrilled to be on the Cape again, but his reasons today have little to do with proving himself healthy and reestablishing his draft position. "I'm now mostly playing for the fun of it," he says. "I'm in a great location and playing with great teammates. What better place is there to be?"

On the Air!

One major lifeline the families have seized is the ability to hear live-action accounts of their son's games on the Internet or over the phone. Karen Curreri listens on the computer every chance she gets and shares the experience with other parents thousands of miles away by emailing them during the game. Jamie Miller, whose son Jay plays for Hyannis, also makes extensive use of the free service. "I've had more fun listening to the games on the telephone!" she gushes, and Kathie Robinson, mother of Hyannis catcher Chris, says that not only does her family log on to listen to every game back home in Canada, but "everybody who follows Chris' career listens too."

The game announcers appreciate the rave reviews almost as much as they do the opportunity to broadcast the games themselves. Virtually all are enrolled in major college communications programs, and they all see their time on the Cape as a chance to develop their skills and add to their resumes.

Guy Benson and Dan D'Uva are the current voices of the Chatham A's, and even as team interns, both knew full well how special it would be to call the games of a Cape League team. When friends alerted them several years ago to the league's impending arrangement for Internet and telephone broadcast distribution, the pair submitted a proposal to the A's to take on the job. "I looked into the future and couldn't pass up the opportunity to try," Benson says, and today they can be seen – and heard – producing and airing the team's pre- and post-game shows, as well as the play-by-play. So successful have they become that even fans attending the games dial in to hear what they have to say.

"We could be doing things with the Fox Network and YES, but we'd rather be here," D'Uva says, and his satisfaction is fully echoed by his broadcast partner. "This is a well-known league that is respected by people who know baseball," Benson says, "and it's in one of the most beautiful places in the country." Is it any wonder, therefore, that they chose the path they did?

Chatham announcer Dan D'Uva prepares for a broadcast.

Peter Frechette understands this thinking perfectly well and has orchestrated a large part of his career accordingly. Coordinating Producer of the popular DVD *Touching the Game: The Story of the Cape Cod Baseball League*, Frechette first got to know the league during his time with the New England Sports Network (NESN), for which he produced the magazine show Front Row among other programs. "Curiosity was what drew us to the league back at NESN," he said, and when he decided to join the ranks of the independents, making a documentary about it was one of the first projects he pursued. "The Cape League is a sporting phenomenon in New England that you hear about and read about, but maybe don't know a whole lot about," he says, and the DVD was conceived to fill that gap.

Frechette's narrator is Boston Herald columnist and sportsradio/TV personality Steve Buckley, who was first introduced to the league while visiting friends in the town of Dennis as a teenager. "It was the most organized game I'd ever seen outside Fenway Park," he says, and he remembers it as being "good eye candy" for a 16- or 17-year-old kid who really liked the sport.

Today, Buckley appreciates the league for its other attributes as well. "Cape League baseball is the baseball you would like to think still exists," he says, and he especially enjoys the many "characters" to be seen at any given game – among his favorites are anthem-singing public address announcers and demonstrative hot dog vendors, both of which he sees as key contributors to the league's old-time flavor. But like so many others, he also values it for being the player proving ground it has become.

"This is a finishing school for amateur baseball," he says, characterizing the league as "the last great platform [for players] to show their talents" before they enter the pros. The organizer of a show-stopping game of his own – his annual Old Time Baseball Game features many top amateur and scholastic players from the area and raises tens of thousands of dollars for charity – Buckley derives particular satisfaction when one of his 'discoveries' (Carlos Peña of the Detroit Tigers, for exam-

Touching the Game producer Peter Frechette (left) and his partners throw out the ceremonial first pitch before a Cape League game. "We don't know whose ball it was that clanged off the screen!" he says.

ple) emerges as a star on-Cape. Thus his interest in the league often is quite personal, and he delights in dedicating at least one column every year to the topic.

Ballyard Chatter

"You have to work hard at being an amateur baseball aficionado in New England, but you don't have to work at Cape League baseball."

– *Steve Buckley, Boston Herald and WEEI Radio*

Play Ball!

Cotuit's Chase Headley anticipates a play. (©2004, Cotuit Athletic Association. Photo by Rick Heath.)

Another Opening, Another Show

The bellwether event on the Cape League calendar is the First Pitch Brunch, at which the teams gather to celebrate the opening of another season, the managers take a moment to outline their expectations, and boosters and media types both mix with the very folks whose fortunes they'll be following all summer long. This particular year, the sun is out, the weather is warming, and optimism rules the roost: after all, no one's yet lost a game, and absolutely anything can still happen!

The same sensibilities rule the roost at various team events as well. The Harwich Mariners, for instance, hosts a cookout at its field for its players, coaches, and host families, and the mood is distinctly upbeat: the sweet aroma of barbeque sauce

Mariners Ryan LaMotta, John Slone, and Jon Aughey add fixin's to their BBQ buns. (courtesy Bob Prew)

floats through the trees under a high summer sky, and knots of laughing people dot the walkways and cluster at the picnic tables on what has turned out to be a picture post-card day.

Falmouth, too, fetes its community with a gathering at The Flying Bridge, a local seafood restaurant, while Wareham hosts an opening barbeque at the Bay Pointe Country Club in nearby Onset. All the teams do it, and the attitude at each event is much the same: this could be the year!

The players are probably the most uncomfortable people at these events, for they're not from around here, and they're full of nervous anticipation as before a first date: How's this going to go? What's it going to be like? I hope I do OK. I'm pretty good; they'll see. I hope I don't embarrass myself! I wonder if they like me? Everyone does his best to make them feel at home, but there clearly is a feeling-out process at work as the players seek some common ground among themselves and with their families-to-be. Wareham president and general manager John Wylde says the difference in atmosphere is palpable between the team's opening barbeque and its closing clambake, by which time meaningful, lifelong bonds have formed between teammates and with the community.

Vim and Vigor

It's mid-June, and the Cotuit Kettleers are holding one of their first practices of the year. But besides working their players out, manager Mike Roberts and his staff are busily trying to forge a single squad out of 23 individuals who hail from nearly as many colleges, and who don't even yet really know each other's name. Complicating matters even further is the fact that some of the players on the field right now will not even be here in two weeks, as they have signed on to play only until the arrival of the several players on Cotuit's formal roster who are still playing in the College World Series.

Crack! Roberts hits grounder after grounder to his infielders, barking out game situations to indicate where they should throw the ball after catching it. *Whack!* The assistant coaches hit fungoes to the outfielders, learning their range and gauging their arm strength. *Whump!* The pitchers throw easily in the bullpen, loosening their arms while still giving their coaches and catchers a taste of what they can do. The expectation is that a unified team will soon emerge, and everyone is eager for the games to begin.

As these Bourne Braves demonstrate, warming up can be fun!

A Game Apart

A large part of Cotuit's practice regimen – and that of the other teams as well – now and all year long involves bunting, baserunning, and quick-handed fielding, "turn back the clock" kinds of skills that reflect the Cape League's use of the wooden bat as much as anything. As a result, many feel baseball here is more "pure" than the game seen either in college, where aluminum bats are standard equipment, or in the pros, where home runs and extra-base hits are seen as keys to victory.

Agree or not, it is clear that Cape Leaguers at least play a different style of baseball than is commonly seen on TV. "Even batting practice doesn't sound the same as it does in the pros," a scout observes in Cotuit one day, and in saying so, he puts his finger – or ear – on one of the most important aspects of Cape League baseball: namely, how much of a big deal using a wooden bat turns out to be.

Rick Oliver, a former first round pick of the Milwaukee Brewers who now works as an agent, says that he didn't understand at first why the pitchers would be so far ahead of the hitters at the season's start. This surprised him because "being a former player, I have some knowledge about the game," he said. "But when I started going year after year, it became very clear that the difference between wood bats and aluminum bats is huge."

Rob Mummau, a scout for the Seattle Mariners, concurs. "Every player is different," he notes, "but it can take maybe half the season to adjust. Many players use wood during the college year at practice just to get used to it."

Wareham outfielder Travis Tully has played in tournaments before using wooden bats, so he is familiar with them coming into the Cape League and really isn't worried about it. Plus, he says, "as a hitter, I try to hit everything the other way anyway, so it doesn't really matter to me." However, a few weeks into the season he is struggling, and says has wished for aluminum at times just to get back on track.

"The first month is really feeling your way," says Harwich's Brent Lillibridge. "You can't really look at batting average; you have to credit the defenses and the pitching too." A veteran of Team USA and the Pan Am games, he believes the baseball is harder here, not in the least because of the consistently high quality of the pitching. "All the guys here have good stuff, and are the best on their college teams," he says. "If you can get past this, then you can take it with you anywhere you go."

The need to adjust to wood serves to depress batting averages and to make long balls relatively hard to come by. Former Orleans manager and current Phillies scout John Castleberry thus encourages players not to worry too much "even if you're only hitting a buck-fifty" because "that's the norm!" Because this is so, Cape League teams play a lot of "small ball," which is to say, they bunt, play hit-and-run, and steal much more often than their counterparts in the pros, which tend to wait for the home run to ride to the rescue.

Hyannis coach Nick Siemasz, who has been in league since the 1970s and has lived through the switch from aluminum back to wood, says the teams now play "real baseball," and like Y-D manager Scott Pickler, he likes what he sees. "It's a different game without the home run, without a doubt," Pickler says, and among other accommodations he makes, "we bunt more frequently all year long."

Later in the season, though, things change as batters begin to abandon what one scout calls "that damned aluminum bat swing." Falmouth coach Marshall Canosa describes this as holding the hands away from the body and taking a big roundhouse cut at the ball, and once hitters figure out that they need to be more compact in order to succeed, they start catching up with the pitchers. At that point, Pickler says, "you need to show them more off-speed stuff and fewer fastballs," and

Brewster's Gaby Sanchez swings the lumber while fans watch from the hill.

Falmouth coach Marshall Canosa directs on-field traffic during practice. (courtesy Dan Dunn Collectables)

that's when the game of cat-and-mouse between pitcher and hitter finally begins.

Now the true prospects will begin separating themselves from the bunch, and the scouts will begin taking a keen interest in the proceedings. Hyannis manager Greg King says the difference between the players who survive and those who don't is "the ability to deal with failure," and we are about to see just who is who.

Rain, Rain Go Away

There is a sumptuous variety about the New England weather that compels the stranger's admiration — and regret. The weather is always doing something there; always attending strictly to business; always getting up new designs and trying them on people to see how they will go. – Mark Twain

It is misting heavily today, the way it can on the Cape, not quite raining, but definitely umbrella weather, and it promises to get worse before it gets better. And yet, several hundred fans are settled into place along the left- and right-field lines, and on the cold, damp aluminum bleachers that glisten behind the dugouts.

What are they all doing here? From the looks of things, the teams will be lucky to play at all, never mind to get in the requisite five innings.[1] But here they are nonetheless, ready to root, root, root for the home team, and then go home happy, win, lose, or drown.

The players, meanwhile, huddle in their dugouts and speak of better days ahead. It is early in the Cape League season – barely a week after opening day – and for many, this is foreign territory indeed. What kind of beach resort is only 60° in the third week of June?

Former Harwich Mariner and major league star Cory Snyder remembers being very surprised by the conditions on the Cape because of how different they are from those he experienced when he played in Alaska. "The weather there was nice all the time," he recalls, "but it can get a little cold on the Cape at night! Especially in Orleans and Chatham, when you're right next to the water."

Foggy, Foggy Dew

The fog, too, makes a dramatic first impression on unsuspecting players. "I've had snow delays and rain delays, but never fog delays!" Hyannis catcher Chris Robinson says. The experience also was something new for former Commodore moundsman and current major leaguer Eric Milton, who remembers well the first time fog caused one of his games

---

[1]In effect, the rules of baseball say the losing team must come to bat at least five times for a game to be considered official and for all statistics to count.

to be scrubbed. "We were in Falmouth," he says, "and it was pretty amazing. The fog rolled in little by little, and the next thing you knew, you couldn't see anything!"

Snyder recalls being fogged out of two or three games during his time on the Cape. "I think I hit three home runs in one game over in Wareham," he says, "and you could barely even see the outfield to see if they went over." As a California kid, Snyder had not seen anything quite like this before. But even local products find the Cape Cod fog to be somewhat unusual.

Roy Bruninghaus grew up in Millbury, Massachusetts, and pitched for Orleans in the 1930s, '40s, and '50s. As a Cape League rookie in 1933, he found himself rather damp to the core one day. "One of my teammates said, 'What's the matter,

The Chatham scoreboard disappears as the fog rolls in.

Player Profile: Chris Robinson

Chris Robinson loosens up before a game.

Hyannis Mets catcher Chris Robinson is one of only a few born-and-bred Canadians in the Cape League. Hailing from Dorchester, Ontario, he opted for baseball over hockey and thus took a path much less traveled by most of his mates.

"I was always backwards for a Canadian," he remembers, "as I played hockey to get ready for baseball, rather than the other way around." A third baseman for much of his youth, he made the switch to catcher because "I like being centrally involved in the game."

Drafted out of high school by the New York Mets in 2002, he was chosen to play for the Canadian Junior National team at the Junior World Championships that summer, and played for the Canadian Senior National Team in the summer of 2003. That same year, he led the Windsor Selects to the Canadian National Championship, and his coaches at the University of Illinois saw to it that he be considered for Cape League play in 2004.

"I get to play with and against the best players in the country," he says, and though he is playing well enough to have been named to the All Star team, he finds the transition to using wooden bats quite frustrating. But, he says, "it is fun as a catcher to watch the batters struggle!"

Robinson is studying sports management with a minor in business, and having been through the draft process once before, he is taking all the Cape League hoopla in stride. "You can't control anything about the draft," he says, and he credits his Illinois coaches for helping him understand that "all you can control is the way you play." So he plays hard every day, and because he does, he receives the league's Daniel J. Silva Sportsmanship Award. Having long ago traded his skates for spikes, he hopes to soon follow his childhood pals now in the NHL into the major leagues of his chosen sport.

Grunie?'" he remembers. "'I said, it's raining!' He said, 'Rain? This is just a mist.' And I said, 'Where I come from, this would be rain!'"

This summer, Robinson and his Hyannis mates traveled to Nantucket to play a game against Y-D, only to have that contest held up three times because of fog. "By the time they called the game, I could only see the center fielder's legs," he says. In typical Cape fashion, the weather everywhere else in the region – including on Nantucket itself – was sunny and clear: only when the teams arrived at the field in the center of the island did they run into problems. Unfortunately, the delays ate up so much time that the teams had to hustle back to town to catch the last ferry home, and the players could not play tourist as well as baseball as they had originally hoped.

This fickle weather is not unusual for Cape Cod and can confound the decision to continue or postpone a given game. Umpire Gary Shingleton tells the tale of a "fog-out" he officiated in Harwich, in which play was stopped in the fifth inning, resumed when the fog lifted, and halted altogether in the eighth when the fog returned.

"The evening prior I was in Cotuit and using sunscreen," he says. "What is that, 20 minutes south? The crew in Harwich that night called the game in the third inning because of fog. When I arrived there [for my game] the following evening, the Harwich GM informed me that the fog had lifted 30 minutes after the umpires suspended play.

But the crew waited 20 minutes and left Whitehouse Field promptly after that time," so the game did not resume. Needless to say, the Mariners were not pleased with this outcome and were not especially happy the next night when the situation repeated itself.

Bearing the previous night's weather pattern in mind, Shingleton constantly interceded with the umpire behind the plate (who also was umpire-in-chief) and at third base, imploring them to take their time before calling the contest. But in the end, the decision had to be made, and no one was surprised when it was unpopular in the Mariner dugout and

Harwich and Chatham players visit during a "fog delay" at Whitehouse Field.

in the stands. "I had the unfortunate task of handling the Harwich manager in the parking lot while my two partners and their wives made a particularly quick exit from the premises. Had I backtracked to the field, my experience would not have been a pleasant one considering the host of Harwich fans I would have needed to pass along the way. It was not the best of evenings!"

It's Not the Heat ...

The flip side of the cold and fog found on the Cape is the heat and humidity that can arise almost instantly in their place. There are days in July and August where it is as sticky on the Bass River as it is along the Potomac, a fact that might surprise the sweaty denizens of our nation's capital but is all too familiar to Cape Codders. For players who come from our country's warmer climes, the soaring of the thermometer can actually be a welcome reminder of home. "90 degrees here is like a spring day back in Texas," says Brewster's Will Rhymes, who hails from Houston and finds it all quite familiar.

Perhaps the ones to feel sorry for are the players from Northern California, where it never seems to get either too cold or too hot. One member of the Y-D Red Sox is observed warming himself by the heat of a citronella torch at a backyard barbeque: a San Francisco native, this poor soul is not used to the Cape's cool early summer evenings, and he's left his jacket at the field. At the same time, he's heard tell of the steamy days to come, and he mutters to himself about this strange world he now inhabits.

Lessons Learned ...

Playing on the Cape provides an excellent opportunity for players to try new things in a setting that may be more liberating than doing so under the watchful eyes of their college coaches. Hitting a baseball has been described as the single hardest thing to do in sports, and pitching one isn't a whole lot easier. So changing one's approach to the game – even when there is virtually no down side to doing so – isn't something anybody takes lightly, especially when full athletic scholarships and possible multimillion dollar contracts are on the line.

Whether it's insight into improving the wood-bat swing or instruction regarding the finer points of fielding, plenty of advice is available to any Cape League player who wants it and is willing to put in the time and effort to learn. "Frankie's getting a million-dollar education from his catching coach here," says Len Curreri, father of Y-D Red Sox star Frank, and observers have commented on how far his footwork has come in the short time he's been on Cape.

... Or Not!

But not everyone is open to input, of course. Y-D recently had a player who never – literally *never* – swung at the first pitch he saw in any given time at bat. Opposing teams quickly figured this out, and from that time forward, pitchers started him off with a fastball right down the middle. As a result, every at-bat began with a count of 0-1, and his batting average began to free-fall.

Club General Manager Jim Martin remembers taking the boy aside after a while to point out the pattern, and to explain the resulting opportunity the player had to feast on those initial fat pitches. "I begged him to swing at the first pitch that night," he recalls, "and even his coach said, 'Son, you've just received some very sound advice, and I'd strongly encourage you to take it.' But all he could say was, 'Sir, I just don't think I can do that,' and sure enough, he couldn't."

Sometimes the college coaches have such firm ideas of their own that succeeding on the Cape only complicates the player's life back at school. Martin recalls a pitcher who had been taught to throw straight over the top but whose fastball, though exceptionally fast, flew straight as an arrow and thus was easy to hit. Noticing that the boy threw three-quarters when playing casual games of catch, Y-D manager Red Wilson had him use that more natural motion when pitching in games too, and the player was "lights-out" effective from that point forward.

The Y-D Red Sox practice before a game.

Unfortunately, when the player returned to school that fall, his coach insisted he also return to the over-the-top motion he had used the year before, even despite the success he had just achieved on the Cape. Predictably enough, the magic did not continue, and when the player rejoined the Red Sox the following summer, he did so with a plea for help.

To Coach, or Not to Coach?

Partly because too many voices can confuse a young player – and possibly alienate a college coach who has a particular regimen in mind – Cape League managers and coaches are relatively hands-off when it comes to changing mechanics unless asked specifically for help. Consequently, "they do more managing than actual coaching," says former major league catcher and current Diamondbacks scout Matt Merullo, who played in the league some 50 years after his grandfather Lennie did.

Chatham manager John Schiffner agrees, saying, "We don't have formal practices; we just do workouts before games." His feeling is that there is so little time off that there isn't much to be gained by forcing players to attend more struc-tured sessions. In addition, many more players now arrive on Cape with weightlifting schedules and summer conditioning requirements in their equipment bags. "They're expected to do their lifting and need to properly rest after a heavy session if they're going to be prepared to play a game," Schiffner says. "So you do limit the time that you can practice. But if a guy is really struggling and is not showing up for the workouts, at a certain point he's told he'd better start coming or it will affect his playing time."

Then there is the question of just how much raw instruction these top-flight college players really need. To that point, Hyannis skipper Greg King notes that "some coaches make them do things their way, but I just fill out the lineup card and let them play." That the players mesh so well on the field

Hyannis manager Greg King "not coaching" his Mets in the batting cage.

after so little practice together is "testament to their natural talent and to their college coaches," King says, and as illustration, he points to such tricky feats of timing as turning a double play. "They've done it so many times that they know just where to feed the ball, and just where to expect it."

Falmouth's Canosa agrees, and points to the increasing crispness of the relay throws from the outfield and the more regular turning of double plays as evidence that the team is starting to gel. "The players are so good that it doesn't take long for them to start working together," he says.

In the end, what the players get out of their time on the Cape depends upon what they put into it. Thus, Bourne Braves infielder Kyle Padgett is finding his stint in the league to be invaluable. "I started as a temp player, so I've been playing not knowing if the coach is going to send me home," he said, "and because I'm from William and Mary College, going against the best pitching from big schools like Georgia Tech has been a big adjustment. But even though I was struggling early on, now I'm beginning to feel like I can play with these guys."

Many players experience a similar sense of accomplishment and find they return to their college teams having dramatically improved. Ron Conte, assistant general manager at Orleans, says that "many don't know they've improved until they get back," and Cotuit general manager Bruce Murphy concurs. "I

tell the players they may not see their improvement here, but
they will when they get back to school," he says. "Back with
the aluminum bat, they will have a different swing, and they
won't be facing Number One pitchers every day." How could
they not be better off for their Cape experience?

Umpires of the Sun

Part of what players learn is how to deal with umpires
other than those they see in their home conferences. In practical terms, the presence of different faces means the existence
of different personalities, different strike zones, and different
degrees of experience calling games played at the consistently
high speed and intensity level seen on the Cape. The ability to
adjust to these variations without issue is critical to the athletes'
success and is closely watched by scouts and managers alike.

Cape League umpires are provided by the ECAC,
a college conference, which polls its officials to gauge
their interest in working summer baseball and then
matches the needs of the league with the schedules of the
interested umpires. Many work only several days or weeks,
and some come from elsewhere in the East by virtue of their
connections to specific conferences that fall under the ECAC
umbrella. Umpire Tim Carey likes this aspect of his summer
job because "it gives us local guys a chance to work with guys
from other places too, and that's a lot of fun."

A stint on the Cape also provides a good test of an umpire's
ability to call a game and handle a crowd, which on any given
night here can be much larger than at a small-college game. A

Cape assignment also fosters a feeling of camaraderie among the officials. Long-time arbiter Nick Zibelli, who worked his first Cape League game in 1974, tells of the times the boss calls everybody up to get together after their games are completed. "You can do that on the Cape because everybody's working so close together," he says. "In other leagues, you might be 70 miles apart."

"The beauty of this league is the ability the players have to make plays," Zibelli says. "The middle infielders are so good – their hands are so quick – and young kids view these guys as if they were major leaguers." But beyond that, he is struck by one other factor. "A player stealing second base once popped up after his slide and said, 'How are you, blue?'" he says. "In other leagues, umpires get a lot of sass every minute of every game, but here it's different."

"It's a privilege and an honor to work this league," Zibelli continues. "After all, if you're going to umpire, you may as well umpire the best."

Ballyard Chatter

"We're playing against major leaguers, only we don't know who they are yet."

– *Mike Costanzo, Hyannis Mets, to teammate Chris Robinson*

"No, we're playing against *Hall of Famers*, only we don't know who they are yet."

– *Robinson to Costanzo in reply*

Outside the Lines

Young fans stand ready for game-time action.

Places to Go ...

Though the competition on the field is certainly the center of attention, much of the appeal of the Cape Cod Baseball League has little to do with baseball itself. For many of the folks on hand – baseball professionals and "civilians" alike – the simple fact that Cape League games are played, well, on Cape Cod is enough to attract them to the cause.

The Cape, of course, is an arm-shaped spit of sand that sticks out into the Atlantic Ocean approximately 60 miles south of Boston, Massachusetts and 60 miles east of Providence, Rhode Island. Because most of the Cape League's on-field staff comes from other parts of the country, they are wholly unfamiliar with the area and all it has to offer, and the opportunity to spend time here is a large part of their decision to come. For her part, Y-D trainer Carrie Ann Saikowski found the Cape to be "much broader than I thought it would be," having mentally equated it with the barrier islands of her native Virginia.

The Cape is known for a wide variety of attractions that include fabulous beaches (Cape Cod Bay, Nantucket Sound, and the National Seashore provide plenty of variety); celebrity visitors (Hyannisport being where the Kennedys famously summered); fresh seafood (Chatham clams perhaps leading the way); scientific research (as conducted by the Woods Hole Oceanographic Institute); theater and the arts (as featured by the likes of the Cape Playhouse in Dennis, the Wellfleet

Harbor Actors Theater, and innumerable Provincetown galleries); and enough mini-golf to satisfy even the most ardent nine year old.

Los Angeles Dodgers' scout Ron Rizzi describes the Cape experience as being "a smorgasbord" with a very eclectic mix of items. "Where else can you walk two blocks from the ballpark to where Rose Kennedy went to Mass every day?" he asks, referring of course to Hyannis. Or drive less than a half-hour (from either Brewster, Chatham, Harwich, or Orleans) to touch the very origins of our nation (the Pilgrims having landed in Provincetown before founding their colony in Plymouth)? Or hop a ferry (from Falmouth) to the famous resort islands of Martha's Vineyard and Nantucket?

Attending a baseball game therefore represents just one of a wide variety of things to do when spending time on the Cape, and yet more than 11,000 people still make their way into Cape League stands on any given day. There must be something good going on here!

... People to Meet

In fact, a Cape League game often is the evening event that follows an afternoon's activities. Jamie Miller, mother of Hyannis Mets outfielder Jay, reported just this sort of double-header after she spied one family cavorting on the beach after lunch and then sitting down the left-field line after dinner.

A recent survey of Cape League fans confirms the family feel of the typical game, as nearly a third of the 260+ respondents said they attend games with their children, friends, or spouse/significant other. And be they fans along the foul line or relatives of the players on the field, they all savor every moment of their time with the game.

Not everyone in attendance is a baseball lifer, of course – one Cotuit fan, for example, said he only became interested in the sport after attending a Kettleers game last summer – but not a night goes by that conversations in the crowd don't

Keene, New Hampshire's Noah Timmer and his dad enjoy a game at Brewster.

center on the wholesome fun and incredible value the Cape League provides. "You can't do *this* at Fenway!" is a frequent refrain as children scamper to retrieve a foul ball, obtain an autograph, play running bases, or play catch *all while the game is going on.* And an accounting is usually made of the major-league expenses for parking, tickets, food, and souvenirs that have been avoided by coming to a Cape League game: parking and tickets here are free (though donations are gladly accepted), the food is inexpensive and plentiful, and the souvenirs are high-quality and reasonably priced. No doubt about it, going to a ballgame on Cape Cod is different than going to one in the Bigs!

Who Are You, and Why Are You Here?

Cape League crowds are largely made up of both vacationers and residents, which sounds wholly unremarkable given the makeup of the Cape's summer population but is significant because it means the league appeals to tourists and townies alike. This puts it into very select company as a featured attraction.

Joe Tassinari falls into both categories, as he lives in Dennis for six months of the year and in Florida for the other six. "I've been coming for 17 years because I love baseball!" he enthuses, explaining that he grew up in East Boston next to a park that had four fields and games on every night. "Two sisters and a brother-in-law went to [Cape League] games 30 years ago, and I just went along," he says, thereby kicking off a life-long personal tradition.

Brad Maltby is another with a long-standing interest in the league. He grew up in Wareham, and remembers the town's Cape League entry as being a big part of his youth. "Chuck Knoblaugh

> **Ballyard Chatter**
>
> "The sound of the ball hitting the bat is more intimate here than in a big ball park, where it is so remote."
>
> – *fan Bill Helene of East Orleans*

and Mo Vaughn ran the clinics, and Gatemen players visited the community many times," he recalls. As a Little League All Star, he played and practiced with the team, and in high school, he played on the Gatemen's home field. "I also used to go to seven or 10 games a year because it was a good place to take a date!" he says. "In those days, you either went to the beach or went to the ballpark, and it was a great night out."

But one doesn't have to reside on the Cape to be captivated by Cape League baseball. Bill Wilhelm lives in Duxbury on Boston's South Shore, which is about a 20-minute drive from the Sagamore Bridge that leads onto the Cape. A former athlete and coach of several schoolboy teams, he is especially appreciative of the quality of play and the congenial atmosphere. "There's a purity about the experience," he says, and as sports director of radio station WATD-FM, he dedicates significant summer air time to the Cape League and encourages listeners to see it for themselves.

Thaddeus Marciano loves it so much that he drives up from Brooklyn – in a car with New York license plates that read 'CCBL' – just to take in Cape League games. "We come just to follow the baseball," he says, and he and his family look forward to seeing former Cape Leaguers as professionals when they play his home-town Cyclones, a class A affiliate of the New York Mets. Meanwhile, he beams as his son Zach serves as the batboy first for Harwich and then for Chatham on two consecutive nights.

John Carpenter's journey is considerably longer but has brought him to the same place as a Cape League baseball fan. Born and raised in the U.K., he came to the U.S. to play soccer for Mount Ida College in Newton. While there, he developed an appreciation for baseball in general, and now that he lives in Plymouth, he knows that "this is true baseball, right here." And so he sits comfortably in his beach chair in Cotuit, just to the right of home plate, and roots as hard as anyone for his adopted home team.

Beach Chairs and Baseball Bats

The beach chair is the seat of choice for many fans in the Cape League, and not only because it is easier on a person's behind than a hard bench for the two-and-a-half or three hours of a typical ballgame. Though all the fields feature bleachers to a greater or lesser degree, there is nothing quite like being able to choose your own sight line and your own seat-mates by plopping down wherever you please.

John Neylon of Watertown, Massachusetts, says "we sit in the same spot by the bullpen so we get familiar with the pitchers and catchers, and the people who are there, who tend to be the same ones all the time." Being at the edge of the action also happens to be convenient for the two pugs he and his wife Diane inevitably bring along, for as much as the dogs love to eat bits of hot dog while sitting in John's lap, there does come a time when they need a "seventh-inning stretch" of their own.

The variety of seats in use is staggering, and quite a bit larger than one ever would have imagined existed. There are Adirondacks, chaise lounges, and camp stools; they're made of plastic, canvas, and fabric; many even feature footrests and drink holders! A Cape League game thus is a study in

Chair today ... gone tomorrow! (courtesy Tom McGinty Photography)

style, a colorful parade of folding furniture that surrounds the green field and ends neatly at the white lines on either edge. The people toting the chairs know there's excitement to be found on both sides of those lines, and they are eager for the festivities to begin.

The 50/50 Raffle

One of the best known off-field attractions at a Cape League game is the 50/50 raffle, a game of chance that derives its name from the fact that the team and the holder of the winning ticket each take home 50% of the kitty. The teams fund a significant portion of their operating budgets in this way, and at especially well-attended games, the pot can top $1500.

Tickets can be purchased singly or in strips – Bourne, for one, even sells them by the "arm's length" and the "wing-span" – and generally are available either at a central location, typically found behind home plate, or from players and volunteers who wander together among the fans. Though the premier prize is a wad of cash, other giveaways include everything from canal cruises to sessions with a local hypnotist, and the crowd anticipates the outcome of the drawing almost as eagerly as they do the outcome of the game.

Orleans pitcher Matt Torra says he always seems to be chosen to work the crowd, but he likes it, and as a result, he's good at it. "It makes the game go faster," he says, and he shows remarkable poise with the little kids as he gives them a free chance to win an autographed ball. All told, prowling the crowd takes about four innings and requires not only making change and counting out the correct number of tickets, but also properly separating the strips so both the customer and the basket are left holding the same set of numbers.

Kids' Clinics

The high point of the summer for any baseball-minded kid on the Cape has to be the weekly clinic that each team puts on. The coaches are the Cape League players themselves, who are hired by the team and use the experience as their summer job. Each day is filled with instruction, drills, Simon Says, and scrimmages, and it's hard to tell who enjoys it more, the player-coaches or the kids.

"We want a single, just a little single!"

On this typical day in Yarmouth, catcher Ben Crabtree juggles baseballs in the bullpen for the six-year-olds, who cannot quite believe their eyes. Meanwhile, manager Pickler waters the infield while talking on his cell phone, then hops on a tractor and traces precise patterns in the dirt. The result is an impeccably manicured field whose rich greens and deep browns mirror the blue sky in depth and intensity, and onlookers know they're part of something special.

The Y-D Red Sox clinics culminate with a rousing game of "egg toss" in which parent pairs off with child, and usually ends up being chided for having broken the egg for not using "soft hands." Sox manager Scott Pickler then heaves eggs up in long high arcs for his players to try to catch. A few do make

The Slip-n-Slide claims a victim.

the play, but most attempt fancy behind-the-back moves that merely result in egg shampoos.

Fortunately, the kids then can clean up by taking repeated trips down a Slip-n-Slide, a water-soaked length of vinyl down which the campers travel on their stomachs, seats, or other available body parts. Pickler seems to take great delight in squirting innocent passers-by as he wets down the slide, and his smile is nearly as wide as the kids'.

Happily, the conclusion of the clinic does not mark the end of the fun, for the relationship that develops between coach and camper continues all summer long. Grins of recognition are exchanged through the backstop when they see each other

Y-D's Sean Gamble and a damp camper.

during practices and games, and the personal connection they enjoy makes for an intimate and powerful experience that will be remembered by both for a lifetime.

Just imagine the excitement of the eight-year-old boy who watches his coach from the clinic drive in the winning run at the All Star game three weeks after posing for a picture at the Slip-n-Slide – and then sees him make his major league debut three years after that! And imagine, too, the excitement the players feel to be the subject of such adoration and attention – they may be Big Men on their college campuses, but this is something different: strangers of all ages, from all over the country, asking for an autograph and a moment, anticipating their greatness to come.

Accessibility, Thy Name is Cape League

This ability to get up close and personal with the players and, indeed, the game itself is one of the most amazing and attractive aspects of the Cape League experience. Somewhere along the line in professional and even major college ball, a divider has arisen between players and the public, to the point

Fans mix with players after a game at Orleans' Eldredge Park.

where no one not in uniform even thinks about going onto the field. But on the Cape, a post-game jaunt around the bases or an on-field autograph session not only is permitted, but is *encouraged.*

These small-time effects are enhanced by others such as the sight of the players, still in uniform, tending to the field or picking up the park after the crowd goes home. All are highly appealing to today's jaded fans, and the familiarity they breed is central to the league's allure.

Meet Mr. Cardinal

Visitors to Eldredge Park in Orleans may notice an odd squawking from time to time as the home team battles the opposition. "Let's go, Card-naaaals!" is the signature call of Mr. Cardinal, who is one of only two mascots in the league (the other being Homer, number 999 in your Falmouth Commodores program).

Mr. Cardinal is the creation of George Hoskey of Eastham, who began leading cheers in 1998 after the team's assistant general manager Ron Conte spotted him enthusiastically refereeing junior hockey in Nauset and invited him to get involved with the team. Actually, Hoskey first volunteered to host a player (a stint that lasted three years), but when he started going to Cardinals games, he noticed that the crowd wasn't making enough noise to suit him.

So it was only natural that he start walking around the park during games, encouraging patrons to more vocally support their team. And being fully committed to the spirit of the thing, he had his mom send his red union suit, and he quickly became a fixture at the field.

In 2001, an anonymous fan donated $1000 for full-blown cardinal finery, which was stitched by two local artists and makes an indelible impression on everyone who sees it. A small boy on a hayride from Paine's Creek Beach to Kate's Ice Cream in Brewster weeks later spoke excitedly about a "chicken" he had seen at a ballgame, but you get the idea!

Mr. Cardinal (right) and pal Homer from Falmouth sign for eager young fans.

Feeding Frenzy: The Players

During the games, players keep their energy levels up by consuming a steady supply of sunflower seeds, gum, Gatorade, and candy bars. But afterwards, standard practice is for each team to cajole a local restaurant, shop, or other club supporter into providing "real" food after each game, home or away. These meals often take the form of a box lunch at the field or in the parking lot. But occasionally someone invites the guys back to the house for a good ol' fashioned barbeque or other furious feast, and the players always appreciate that little touch of home.

In late June, the Y-D Red Sox descend upon one unsuspecting household that has been generous enough to invite the whole gang – players, coaches, volunteers; *everyone* – to the house for a feeding in the first degree: lasagna, meatballs, spiral ham, baked beans, tossed salad, apple pie, ice cream: the works! The game ends around a quarter to eight in dramatic fashion, as the Sox win on a suicide squeeze in the bottom of the ninth; by eight-fifteen, 23 uniformed ballplayers crowd the backyard, lining the picnic benches with heaping plates of food and guzzling sodas by the gallon.

Though traveling in different cars, most of the players arrive at nearly the same moment, and the hungry horde hurdles the post-and-rail fence out front like an invading army. They are still in uniform, and neighbors watch from their windows as a wave of red laps over the lawn, flows around the house, and pools in the back yard: let the eating begin! Pitcher Brett

Harker later tells host parent Paul McCracken, "I am beyond full," and a good time is had by all.

Later that summer, the Brewster Whitecaps repair to the home of Bob and Linda Riedl, long-time members of the team's support squad who host a cookout every year at their house in the woods. There are hamburgers and hot dogs aplenty, but also clam bisque and the most tender steaks on

The Y-D Red Sox enjoy a home-style meal with a young fan.

the planet. Already impressed by the instructions they received earlier to park their cars between the tennis courts and the swimming pool, the players are not quite sure what to make of this gustatory largesse, but they all appreciate the effort and welcome the opportunity to eat somewhere other than the ballyard.

Gatemen coach and former infielder Casey Lambert – until recently a Colorado Rockies farmhand and now aspiring to play in the Boston Red Sox system – enjoys his 'lobstah' at Wareham's annual end-of-year clambake and barbeque.

Feeding Frenzy: The Fans

The players are not the only ones who enjoy a good meal, as the fans, too, have a taste for the special. Well before the song urges "buy me some peanuts and Cracker Jack," the lines form at the concession stand, and the race is on to see which finishes first, the game or the food.

> **Ballyard Chatter**
>
> "A Snickers, two Airheads, a hot dog, pizza, a soda ..."
> – 7-year-old girl ordering for her family in Chatham

Short-bankrolled as they always are, the teams carefully consider how much they buy for any given game: too much and they risk it going bad; too little and they leave concession money on the table. This is a balancing act that sometimes can leave fans high and dry, as stocks can and do run out before high-scoring or extra-inning games – which run longer than is typical – come to an end.

Experienced grazers guard against this eventuality by lining up early and laying in a supply of their own. But the true experts also know their local fare and choose their poisons accordingly: a hot dog on a grilled, buttered bun in Bourne; a bowl of chili in Brewster; a Mariner's Sundae in Harwich; a sausage, pepper, and onion sub in Falmouth; a package of trail mix in Hyannis.

But you'll never find anything quite like the Slider that's available only in Yarmouth – unless it's the Hurler – for a burger served on a sliced, grilled donut seems not to have caught on anywhere else! In fact, it's not as bad as it sounds, though it quite literally is not for the faint of heart. And creator Bob

Phillips puts on a wonderful show when encouraging his customers – especially those under the age of 12 – to "upgrade" from traditional burger fare. Y'all come!

The Call to the Bullpen

Funny foods are not the only things you see at Cape League fields that you don't see at other baseball locales. For example, in most major league ballparks, a manager wanting to warm up a relief pitcher generally does so by calling down to the bullpen on phone installed in the dugout for that specific purpose. But on the Cape, some of the fields don't even have true dugouts, let alone telephones.

Consequently, it is not unusual to see the pitching coach or manager jump off the bench and gesticulate wildly to his

Burger innovator Bob Phillips and 'victims' Ali and Ashley Russo of Weston, Mass.

relievers to indicate who should get loose or to inquire about their readiness to enter the game. Some use special signals to ask their questions: Hyannis coach Jerry Zulli, for instance, puts his cap on backwards to find out "is he ready yet?" But it is also not unusual to hear the relievers ask themselves after all that, "Do you have any idea what he wanted?" and then have somebody run to the dugout to find out.

Sometimes technology comes to the rescue in the form of walkie-talkies, one half of which resides on the bench and the

A Commodore warms up while a young fan looks on.

other in the bullpen. Most times, though, someone gets a work-out running back and forth to deliver the salient messages – or to bring back napkins so the relief corps can clean itself up after eating the occasional smuggled pizza!

She Loves Me, She Loves Me Not

Sometimes the messages being relayed have more to do with romance than relief pitchers. Stories abound about bullpen and dugout extras who spend their time scanning the crowd for attractive females – the players are, after all, young, single, and a long way from home – and then conspiring to meet them. Sometimes all this requires is arranging to sell 50/50 tickets in a certain section of the ballpark, or maneuvering past many post-game autograph seekers in order to sign for a particular little brother or sister. Other times, their baseball skills come in handy, and this night in Harwich, a Brewster pitcher writes his teammate's name and cell phone number on a ball, and throws a perfect strike to a gaggle of girls in the stands in the hopes of arranging a post-game rendezvous.

Whatever the outcome, this scheme already has worked better than one did for Falmouth's Barry Gunther, who spied a gorgeous redhead among the fans, duly annotated a baseball, and asked a small boy standing nearby to deliver it for him. Unfortunately, the boy gave the ball to the wrong girl, and Gunther found himself having to shout "Get it back! Get it back!" to save himself from some unwanted female attention.

The fans themselves often have tender tales to tell as well. Kelly and Becca Pulju are spending part of their honeymoon at Eldredge Park in Orleans, and when they're not busy gazing into each other's eyes, they are happily watching the home-team Cardinals play the Hyannis Mets. "We go to a lot of town-league games back home in Minnesota," says Becca, and they decided to bop over from Provincetown simply because they're big baseball fans. "We wanted to go to Fenway," Kelly jokes, "but this was a little cheaper!" And on this beautiful early-summer evening, with gulls wheeling overhead and Cardinals circling the bases below, they know they made the right decision.

Player Profile: Scott Lonergan

Scott Lonergan is a rangy right-handed pitcher for the Brewster Whitecaps who grew up near San Diego in Poway, California. The prototypical Southern California kid, "I surfed a lot and played every sport under the roof," he says, including beach volleyball and snowboarding. But baseball was always front-and-center in his life, and he remembers that "my older brother played baseball too and pushed me to get better."

Lonergan says he was on the small size as a youth, but he hit a growth spurt in high school – during which he also played varsity basketball and football – and after a stellar junior year, "I opened a lot of eyes." *Baseball America* rated him the 82nd best player in the nation as a senior, and after graduation, he was drafted by his home-town San Diego Padres. Though he opted not to sign in favor of attending Santa Clara University, he did work out at Qualcomm Stadium and told the team, "draft me in four years, and I'll sign, and I won't even care for how much!"

Unfortunately, a blood clot in his freshman year required surgery and cost him both his college season and his first opportunity to play for Brewster. However, it did teach him how to better put athletics in the context of life, and wanting to make best use of his enforced down time, he took a full load of classes during the summer of his recovery and every quarter thereafter. Consequently, he says, "I'm a red-shirt freshman on the field, but a junior in the classroom."

Now back on the field, Lonergan describes his recent performance as "erratic," though perhaps understandably so given his health history. "[My coaches] don't know which Scott they are going to get," he says, and he worries his inconsistency belies the appreciation he has for the scholarship he received even though he was hurt. This is a young man who knows how privileged he is to be able to compete for a spot in pro ball, and how long the odds are of actually making it. Thus, he is pursuing his marketing degree with the same intensity as he is his former standing as a starting pitcher, a role he prefers to relieving because of the predictable schedule it entails. "It's hard to know how much throwing to do when you don't know when you'll be playing," he says.

The Grind

Falmouth GM Chuck Sturtevant and Manager Jeff Trundy deep in pregame conversation

The Beat Goes On

Whether to spend time with the Cape League is not one of the harder life decisions a person has to make, for the scenery is beautiful, the competition is tough, and the longest possible road trip – from Wareham to Orleans, or vice versa – covers only 48 miles. Of course, weekend traffic can turn this jaunt into a marathon, but all 10 franchises and plenty of attractions are within easy theoretical reach.

Fan Diane Neylon likes going to road games because it lets her keep an eye on her "boys" whenever her family's schedule doesn't align with her team's. "It's a disappointment when there's no home game on a weekend," she says. "If it's a Friday night home game and [my husband] John doesn't get down in time, then we miss it. The Saturday game probably is somewhere else, and the Sunday game might be at 5 o'clock, by which time we've gone home. So we do go to away games on some weekends." John doesn't argue because he finds visiting the other parks to be a nice change of pace. "Plus," he says, you can plan other things around it, like going out to eat or meeting somebody."

Unfortunately for the players and scouts, the free time to make these sorts of arrangements turns out to be a rare and precious commodity. Most of the players have jobs (as do all of the scouts!), and between working in the morning, going to practices in the afternoon, and attending games in the evening, they don't have many opportunities to explore their surroundings or make plans to socialize away from the ballyard. Consequently, Y-D infielder Wes Hodges in mid-July can only lament, "My parents are coming next week and they'll want to know where the good places are to go – and I'll have no idea!"

Work Before Play

Though players no longer are required to have a job while on Cape, they still are encouraged to work, and most of them do. In many cases, they take care of the fields or work as councilors and coaches in the kids' clinics. But local businesses regularly open their doors to the players and invite them to stock shelves at the Stop-and-Shop supermarket (as San Diego's Mark Loretta did while playing for Falmouth), make sandwiches at the town deli (as Anaheim's Tim Salmon did during his time with Cotuit), or dig cart paths at the local golf course (as Oakland's Barry Zito did when in Wareham).

"The first summer I was [on Cape] I was fortunate enough to work at Friendly's," says pitcher Eric Milton. "The bad thing was that they called me the 'salad girl' because I stocked the salad back in the freezer every day." Will Clark, meanwhile, worked at Jim Perkins' gas station, an experience that forced him to "figure out how to work during the day and play ball at night." And Boston Red Sox star Jason Varitek was responsible for doing his team's laundry during his first year in Hyannis. "I had to be at the laundromat at 7am to wash all the unis and clean up the clubhouse," he remembers in the DVD *Touching the Game*, and it was there that the seeds no doubt were planted for the reputation he enjoys for taking good care of the attendants in his major league clubhouse.

Ex-Mariner Cory Snyder believes having a job is one of the greatest take-aways of the Cape League experience. "I like the work thing because it gets you out of the house and doing things, and teaches the kids a work ethic," he says. "Sometimes these days everything is given to athletes; I like the aspect of having them work for something because they're going to be better off in the end." Snyder himself delivered groceries to local restaurants and appreciated the connection with the community the job gave him. "Because I delivered to different restaurants in Harwich, they all knew me," he recalls. "It was nice when they'd say 'Way to go, man; good luck tonight.' It was like being part of a big family, and that was neat."

Tending the field in Chatham (courtesy Tom McGinty Photography)

A's manager Schiffner looks back fondly on that part of his experience as a player in the league in the 1970s, and he remembers well having to work before practices and games. "Back when I was playing, there weren't a lot of 'count the number of seagulls at the beach' kinds of low-maintenance jobs," he recalls. "I was a night watchman at Saquatucket Harbor, but I fell asleep one night, and somebody stole a boat! I lost that job," he now says with a laugh, but he knows how tough it was to fit it all in and marvels at the differences he sees today. "Now, you've got to make sure that these kids have ample time to eat before the game and make sure they are there in time to get a full trainer-oriented stretch," he says. "When I played, you'd get to the ballpark and what was your warmup? Stretch, run, throw! And that was it, let's play." But the basic grind remains the same, and the players today are no more accustomed to it than their counterparts were in years past.

"Ground Hog Day"

This feeling of regimentation and routine is something of a new sensation for many of the players, who certainly work hard during their college seasons but do not play games every day and do not face the same high level of competition every time out. Brewster Whitecap Scott Lonergan describes the feeling as being in *Ground Hog Day*, a reference to the Bill Murray movie of the same title in which the lead character wakes up every morning only to discover he is reliving the day before.

Snyder argues that, in baseball terms, this isn't necessarily a bad thing. "We were working during the day and playing at night, and really didn't have a whole bunch of time off," he remembers. "But that was fine because playing every single night is what got me prepared to play pro baseball for so long."

Snyder and others view the need to cope with a routine as being a very important part of the Cape League experience. In the pros, "you've got to get yourself up every single night, play 110%, and be ready to go," Snyder says. "In college, you play maybe three or four games per week, and usually one or two of those are doubleheaders." Adjusting to this new way of life therefore is a very important part of learning to be a ballplayer.

The Cape League recognizes the scope of this adjustment and does build several days off into its schedule. For sure, this is done to allow for the rescheduling of rained-out games, but it also gives the players a much-needed break, and allows the players' families to plan their own visits to the Cape at a time their sons may be free to visit with them.

Harwich Mariner Brent Lillibridge is fortunate in that he has been able to use these days to do a lot of fishing, right in the bay off the beach, and Brewster Whitecap infielder Will Rhymes, also excited about all the water he saw when he arrived on Cape, is hoping to go surfing before the season is over. (Note: he never does get the chance, but his teammate Scott Lonergan does manage to borrow a board at Nauset before discovering how much colder the ocean is there than back home outside San Diego!)

Cotuit pitcher Cody Evans and third baseman Chase Headley, who are housemates as well as teammates, are looking forward to doing some serious exploring, but five weeks into the season, all they have time for is a Hyannis Harbor cruise – a nice way to spend a few hours to be sure, but hardly the beach blanket adventure they may have been hoping for. Evans does eventually make it to Martha's Vineyard, where he has a good time buzzing around on a rented scooter with his girlfriend.

Y-D's Ben Crabtree works on his swing.

But perhaps more typical of the players' rare day off is the afternoon he spends at the mall with his host family, playing videogames and otherwise just taking a break from what by now is beginning to feel like a grind.

So Close and Yet So Far

The Wareham Gatemen spend one of their off days at Fenway Park in Boston, where they are granted early entrance to watch batting and fielding practice before the Red Sox play the Oakland Athletics – or rather, to watch the former Cape League stars working out on the field below. The list is a long one and includes such big names as Jason Varitek, Barry Zito, Mark Mulder, Bill Mueller, Adam Melhuse, and Kevin Millar. But even though the Gatemen have the run of the park – including access to the new Green Monster seats perched atop Fenway's famous left field wall – the most exciting part about of their day is the moment they each realize *those guys down there* were standing *right where we are* only a few years ago.

This outing is the handiwork of Wareham club president and general manager John Wylde, who makes this special arrangement every year and doesn't even stay for the ballgame that follows. His satisfaction derives from the success of his former charges at the highest levels of their chosen sport – Zito, for example, wore a Gatemen uniform in 1997 and '98 – and the opportunity he has to bring his next group of potential stars to the very threshold of their lifelong dream. Then he quietly slips away and leaves his team to ponder the possibilities.

The dream is clearly visible on the players' faces as they look at the emerald green field before them: they are literally *that close* to being where they want to be and fairly ache to make the transition. Phillies' scout John Castleberry validates the feeling later by reminding the Cape League All Stars that many major

Wareham's Travis Tully surveys Fenway Park from atop the famous Green Monster. Accustomed to the parched fields of his native Texas, he was surprised by the length of the Fenway grass.

league players "were sitting where you're sitting and thinking what you're thinking." And while all that physically separates the Cape Leaguers from the big leaguers right now is a short fence and about 30 feet of infield, everyone present knows that the true distance is a lot longer than that, and is better measured in terms of emotional growth and playing experience than in feet and inches.

Scouts & Scouting

Major league scouts know this too, and a primary reason they come to the Cape is to gauge how ready, willing, and able a player may be to embark on his journey through the pros. Sure, they are here to observe and quantify the performances on the field, but, Arizona's Matt Merullo says, "we watch how guys prepare to play, not just how they play" to get a sense of how committed they are to doing what they need to do.

Generally speaking, scouts view Cape duty as being a plum assignment, for the proximity of the fields, the high caliber of play, and the easy availability of numerous recreational opportunities make their working environment attractive indeed. For his part, Merullo is on hand to administer a standardized psychology test to the players in which Arizona has an interest — a task he doesn't especially relish but also doesn't resist because "it's my ticket to the Cape."

Relatively few scouts are present early in the season, largely because, as has been noted before, many top prospects are still involved in the College World Series and haven't yet arrived on

Cape. A month into the proceedings, however, their numbers are noticeably increased, and radar guns sprout behind home plates around the league like mushrooms following a spring rain. Pitch speed is a prime metric for scouts seeking live arms – and that's all of them – and it has been postulated that so many guns are energized that a fan can heat his hot dog simply by sticking it into the concentration of beams.

Pregame practice for scouts is a time to catch up with old friends even as batting stances and pitching mechanics are observed and noted down. Gossip is freely exchanged as they chat about who now works for whom, which players are worth a look, and who else from the scouting organization will be coming down. As the weeks go by, regional scouts are supplemented and replaced by national cross-checkers, and the pre- and post-game conversations focus more on contract options and draft possibilities than job openings and restaurant menus.

The league itself is serious about supporting the scouts as they seek new talent: this may begin with the sheets of daily player statistics that are routinely given to fans as they enter the park, but it surely extends to the habit Cape League teams have of announcing their starting pitchers three days in advance, information that allows the scouts to efficiently plan their itineraries.

"This is the best run amateur league in the country," says L.A. Dodgers scout John Barr, "and we get to see top college players compete against each other on a daily basis for an entire summer." This year, the league is trying something new to even further enhance the scouts' experience. Responding to requests received from major league baseball during the off-season, it is orchestrating a series of special "Scouts Days," during which each team is setting aside time before a home game so participating players can run formal 60-yard sprints for time. This gives the scouts a useful baseline metric that they can factor into their player evaluations, and obviates the need for the written permission they need to do this during the regular college season. The league also is supplying a box lunch, further endearing itself to the scouts, who move on their stomachs like an army.

Scouting reaches a crescendo at the All Star game, when flocks of observers arrive from multiple levels of the scouting organizations of every major league team. This year, word is that some 70 scouts are on hand, a remarkable number considering that there are only 30 major league teams. A few lucky

Major league scouts – younger and older – watch players participate in Scout's Day activities.

players receive invitations to work out for these clubs in the days following the game, and the stakes for which everyone is playing suddenly become more real. We really are just *that* close to making it, the players' eyes say. I can't mess up now!

Y-D catcher Frank Curreri already has been drafted, by Arizona, and is now waiting for a contract offer. The Diamond-backs are waiting to see how he does on the Cape before committing to a figure, but they are eager to sign him; meanwhile, he's inclined to go back to school but of course is excited about the chance to turn pro. Besides conducting his psych tests, Matt Merullo is here to maintain and mentor Curreri as a pro prospect, and to keep the D-backs apprised of his progress and mindset – both of which are advanced considerably when the news breaks that Curreri has been named to the East Division All Star squad.

Hey Now, You're an All Star

The All Star game is the high point of the Cape League season. Taking place about two-thirds of the way through the schedule, it features teams representing the league's East and West divisions and can attract more than 7000 people. "I went to the All Star game in '94 in Orleans," says Boston Herald columnist and radio/TV personality Steve Buckley, and "I was mesmerized by the festival setting."

ESPN personality Peter Gammons describes the game and its surrounding hoopla as "the essence of the Cape League," and he groups it with the famous Falmouth Road Race as "the two big sporting events on the Cape." The game itself is held after the season's midpoint – the traditional timing of the major league version – not only to allow time for the cream to rise to the top in terms of on-field accomplishment, but also to maintain the players' interest and energy levels as they wear

ESPN's Peter Gammons chats with Commodores Joey Metropoulos and Darryl Lawhorn at the 2003 All Star game. Both players were drafted in 2004, Metropoulos by Toronto and Lawhorn by Arizona. (courtesy Dan Dunn Collectables)

down after playing six straight months of college and Cape
League ball.

The All Stars themselves are chosen by the managers of
the 10 teams, who meet the week before the game and discuss
the candidates position by position. Being chosen is a crowning moment for the players and sets them up for a special day
filled with honors, celebration, and fun. But the occasion is
noteworthy for those who are not selected as well, for it gives
them a day off from everything including practice, and thus is
the ideal time for family and friends to come for a visit.

This year's game is being hosted by Orleans, and the day
starts with a brunch at which the teams, the league, and the
league sponsors pay tribute to the athletes' achievements. Following the introduction of the players and the presentation
of their All Star plaques and uniforms, John Castleberry
encourages the honorees to absorb more than merely baseball
lessons during their time on the Cape. "The most important
thing to take away is the life experience you're getting here," he
says, and he points to the lasting impact they're having on their
respective communities as evidence that there is more going
on here than meets the eye. "You don't realize how you touch
people's lives," he says, but he knows from experience that
they will come to appreciate it more than they can imagine.

After the brunch, the festivities move to the field, where
the home run hitting contest and an autograph session are the
first orders of business. In a nice touch that echoes and honors
the league's town-team foundation, the catcher for the contest

is provided by nearby Nauset High School, and he seems to enjoy the ensuing moon shots as much as anyone. Perhaps the only people to see a dark side to the proceedings are the three Y-D pitchers who are standing at the back of the crowd and are flinching each time a long ball is struck.

Y-D pitchers Justin Meier, Daniel McCutchen, and Blake Holler 'enjoy' the All Star home run hitting contest.

A short while later, the batting and infield practices are complete, and the game finally begins. The day is cold and rainy, yet the teams charge onto the field as if the championship of the world is at stake. However, the suspense is quickly shattered as Curreri hits a two-run home run in the first inning, and the East goes on to rout the West, 13-0. "Other than the brunch and the home run contest," says West team (and Hyannis) catcher Chris Robinson. "the All Star game was almost anti-climactic." Still, the event is a rousing success for the estimated 4500 fans, scouts, and agents who jam into Eldredge Park despite the weather, and the players are left a bit dizzy from the experience.

Brewster's Will Rhymes, the once and former temporary player, finds it to be "a weird day, with all these people wanting autographs." Curreri also finds it a bit surreal, especially after he is named Most Valuable Player for the East. But he is helped by the fact that he grew up only about 50 minutes away in the Boston suburb of Weymouth, and a contingent of 30 or so friends, family, and teammates from the University of Massachusetts have driven down to support him in his All Star appearance. "They made the trip for this special occasion, so I'm glad I was able to do something to give them a treat for being here," he says.

Curreri's performance is particularly sweet because after starting the season like a house afire, he's been in something of a slump as of late. Superstitious as any athlete, he blames his recent woes on having heeded the pleas of his mother Karen and host mother Betsy David to clean up his "scruffy" look before he and the other All Stars visited Fenway Park. But Karen has brought several good-luck charms to All Star game — a new embroidered wrist band and a toy puppy that was a favorite when he was small — and evidently, now all again is well.

Among those who have noticed are the higher-ups in the Arizona Diamondbacks organization, who ring father Len Curreri's cell phone barely 10 minutes after Frank's All Star game honors are bestowed. The D-backs wish to meet to talk about their contract proposal, and while everyone is excited about the development, Frank himself seems to be taking it all in stride. "All the players here are better than many I'd be playing [in the minors] against in Montana or somewhere," he says, and besides, he knows that a strong finish will only enhance his standing as a prospect — and if somehow it doesn't, he can always just return to school. Still, having to choose whether and when to turn pro isn't easy. "I'll play the next few weeks and then decide," Frank says.

The season resumes the next day as if nothing special has happened, and it is such an ordinary day that it stands in stark contrast with the day before. "I knew this would be the hardest game to be sharp for," catcher Chris Robinson says afterwards, but for him, there is a distinct silver lining. "I told my teammates that whoever this lefty is, he won't be better than the two I faced last night!" he says.

Player Profile: Frank Curreri

Karen, Frank, and Len Curreri in a family portrait prior to the All Star Game in Orleans.

A product of Weymouth, Massachusetts, Frank Curreri is one of only a handful of local players in the Cape League. A catcher with the Y-D Red Sox, he is on the verge of his junior year at the University of Massachusetts at Amherst, and is the regular center of attention of untold numbers of friends and relatives who journey down Route 3 to watch him play.

A hockey player from a very early age, Curreri picked up baseball as a summer sport because of a family rule that required all of the Curreri children to play one sport per season. First placed behind the plate to replace an injured teammate, he quickly realized he loved to be in the middle of the action and looked forward to handling the ball on every play. Despite his successes on the diamond, he still considered hockey his first sport and, according to his father Len, was working hard to become the sort of offensive-minded defenseman as long-time Boston Bruins star Ray Bourque. Thus it was somewhat surprising that he was recruited to play *both* sports by interested colleges. Ultimately, he picked UMass because the school has a catching coach under whose watchful eye Frank can improve his game.

On the Cape, all Curreri has done is spend most of the season contending for the league lead in hitting (finally finishing with a team-best average of .293, with two homers and 15 RBI), homer in the Cape League All Star game, be named MVP for the East team at that showcase event, lead the league in on-base percentage (.432), help his team win the league championship, and receive the league's Best New England Pro Prospect Award. This all allows him to complete his summer with the Missoula Osprey, the Pioneer League affiliate of the Arizona Diamondbacks, who picked him in the 41st round of the 2004 major league draft this June and signs him two days after the Cape League season ends.

With the big game now behind them and just a few weeks left in the schedule, players for the first time begin to talk meaningfully of going home. Many are tired, hurt, and homesick, and they often now struggle to maintain their focus.

"The good coaches will ask about the players' commitment, and will remind them that they came to play, and stay, and finish," says Orleans assistant general manager Ron Conte. "That's why a league like this is so important: it begins weeding out who really wants to play."

Conte, in fact, would like to take each player aside and ask them the point-blank question: "why in the world would you want to be a major league player?" Noting the excessive travel, the intense focus, and the negative impact on family life a pro career necessarily entails, he wonders if his charges really understand just what they're getting themselves into.

"The guys who succeed, they don't do anything but baseball," he notes, and with the grind now taking its toll, the scouts are seriously evaluating the size of their prospects' "heart" and the amount of contract money to offer. Several deals are made, and the newly-minted professionals pack their bags to embark on their new careers. Their teammates, meanwhile, gear up for their final push to the post-season, which is the next item on the league's competitive agenda.

Ballyard Chatter

"The quality of baseball [on the Cape] is every bit as good as it is in the South Atlantic League, maybe even a little bit better. These are the cream-of-the-crop college players, and the South Atlantic League has a lot of high school kids who were taken in the previous year's draft."

– *Allan Simpson, Editor-in-Chief, Baseball America*

The 'Second Season'

Playoff passions on display in the championship round

Down to the Wire

Cape League pennant races have a wonderful habit of coming right down to the wire, and the season of 2004 is no exception. With one week to play, fully seven teams of the 10 in the league still harbor realistic hopes of reaching the playoffs – the so-called "second season" – and despite exhaustion, injuries, and a hankering to go home, most are putting up a furious fight to the finish. At one point, Wareham wins nine out of 10 and beats Hyannis to move into second place in the West, and Orleans wins seven games in a row to challenge Brewster for the second spot in the East.

Teams play hard to be the runner-up because the top two teams in each division play each other in the first round of playoffs. The standings are determined using a point system in which two points are awarded for each win, and one for each tie – and ties do occur because half the ballfields do not have lights. Every effort is made to at least complete a full inning before halting a game due to darkness, but there is a natural limit to how long games can go on.

The point system and the existence of ties both are factors this particular summer: in the second-to-last game of the regular season, Orleans at Y-D is called with some controversy due to darkness, and since the game is tied, each team takes home one point. The Red Sox have already clinched first place, but the Cardinals need every point they can earn to help them in their desperate struggle with Brewster for second-place honors, and thus a place in the playoffs. The way things turn out, that missing point costs them their post-season, for when all is said and done, they finish third, a single point behind the Whitecaps.

Meanwhile, over in the West, Cotuit and Hyannis enter the final game of the season in a flat-footed tie for second, and face each other at Hyannis knowing that the winner will face first-place Falmouth in the playoffs, and the loser will go home. Adding to the tension is the fact that the two teams both play in the Town of Barnstable[1], and thus are bitter franchise rivals. This means little to the players themselves, who until a few weeks ago were hard-pressed to find either community on a map, but for team officials and volunteers, it adds a whole other dimension to the proceedings on the field.

Blue Moon Rising

A gorgeous full moon – the second in this particular July – hangs large over Wareham's Spillane Field, where the Gatemen are hosting the visiting Hyannis Mets in a battle for second place in the West. Wareham has been on a roll of late and has charged from the depths of the division to challenge for a place in the playoffs. The Mets, on the other hand, have been struggling at the same time, and the game today promises to be hotly contested.

---

[1] The Town of Barnstable is Cape Cod's largest and consists of the Villages of Barnstable Village, Centerville, Cotuit, Hyannis, Marstons Mills, Osterville, and West Barnstable – and if that's not confusing enough, then consider the fact that the entire Cape is situated inside the County of Barnstable!

Wareham takes a 1-0 lead in its half of the first on an RBI single by Mike Bell, and Hyannis comes right back to tie in the second on a home run by designated hitter Mike Costanzo that sails over the 400-foot marker in dead center field. The Hyannis Web site the next day cites Wareham president and general manager John Wylde as recalling the last slugger to clear that spot to be former Gateman and Seton Hall first baseman Mo Vaughn. So it is clear that something more than merely a tight ballgame is taking place before the 1628 people in attendance.

In the middle of the third, Wareham rallies for two more runs, but not before the sprinkler system suddenly turns itself on. Play is halted, and for the next 20 minutes, we wait while someone tracks down the key to the maintenance shed that houses the shutoff valve. Oddly enough, the sprinklers in Brewster this evening also spring to life in precisely the same way, and coming on the heels of the inadvertent beaning of a Cotuit hitter the night before and a "skunk delay" in Orleans the night before that, the Mets have to be feeling some greater power is at work.

By the bottom of the eighth, the score is tied at three, and the momentum is shifting in Hyannis' favor. But a walk, a single, a double steal, and a wild pitch give Wareham its fourth run before a misfired squeeze bunt and a fly ball end the inning. And before the Mets can even leave the field, fireworks involving the home plate umpire result in the ejection of Costanzo, by now the Mets pitcher, and Hyannis manager

Greg King, who had rushed to his player's defense. The game then ends with three quick Hyannis outs, and Wareham moves into second place on the strength of its 4-3 win.

Winner Take All

Scant days later, Hyannis finds itself tied for second with hard-charging Cotuit, several points ahead of Wareham, which has been bitten by the injury bug and has fallen off the pace. It is the last day of the regular season, and the winner of this game will advance to the playoffs. Much therefore is on the line, and given that most of the participants have been playing since March, victory most likely will come to the team that can better overcome its exhaustion.

More than 2000 people are on hand in Hyannis to witness this Battle of Barnstable, and the action on the field does not disappoint. Cotuit scores once in its half of the second inning, and Hyannis immediately comes back to tie. Cotuit scores again in the fourth, and Hyannis ties it in the sixth on a Costanzo sacrifice fly.

Cotuit plates another in the seventh inning to take a 3-2 lead, and then the fun begins. In the eighth, with both daylight and Hyannis' playoff hopes on the wane, Costanzo launches a two-run home run to dead center field and gives the Mets a 4-3 lead, their first of the day. A two-way player, Costanzo moves from first base to the mound in the top of the ninth and proceeds to retie the game by dropping a low throw while covering first on the inning's initial play, throwing the ensuing sacrifice bunt into center field while trying to get the lead runner at second, walking the next man to load the bases, and then uncorking a wild pitch to allow the tying run to score.

The crowd is hoarse from cheering and is on the verge of contracting the bends from all the ups and downs it has experienced so far. It is clear to everyone that this is yet another Cape League game in which absolutely anything can happen, and as if to underscore this point, the Cotuit catcher overthrows his pitcher during the pre-inning warm-ups at the same instant his shortstop overthrows the first baseman. No harm is done, but strange forces surely again are at work.

So it comes as no surprise to anyone when, in the last half of the tenth, Costanzo hits a long double with a man on, and a perfect throw from the outfield nails the runner at the plate. Nor is it a shocker when the next batter singles and Costanzo himself scores the game-winning run. Somehow it is fitting that this intense young man with the ready smile and love for the game should take center stage on this important day, when the keys to victory had more to do with heart than muscle.

Playoff Pain and Pleasure

And so it is that the playoffs begin. Having outlasted chief rivals Wareham and Cotuit, Hyannis moves on to play Falmouth for the right to represent the West Division in the championship series; meanwhile, in the East, Y-D squares off against Brewster, which made a late move on first place only to be beaten 7-2 by the talented Red Sox in the season's final week.

At this point, playing the game is the least of the players' problems. "We're tired, we're sore, and we do want to go home," says Y-D catcher Frank Curreri, who has taken a particular pounding as of late. But he, his teammates, and his opponents want to go home *winners*, and it is a mistake to assume his honest comments mean anyone is less than fully committed to the championship cause.

"Teams gear up big-time for the playoffs," says Baseball America editor-in-chief Allan Simpson, "but at the same time, they are itching to get home. They've had a long college season, and they stepped immediately into their summer league. But come the playoffs, they turn the juices back up a little and say 'let's get this thing done!'"

Falmouth coach Marshall Canosa confirms that his Commodores don't want to go home until they get what they came for. "After starting 0-5, they know what they can do," he says. "Peter Gammons has said we have the most prospects of any Cape League team, and our players read the papers each day about their accomplishments. So anything less than a championship would be disappointing."

Let the Games Begin

As the post-season begins, the players must find a way to forget their aches and pains and overcome their mental fatigue. This isn't easy, and it doesn't help when their girlfriends in the stands are heard counting down the number of outs remaining until the game – and the season – ends.

But there is something rejuvenating about the playoff atmosphere, and after several weeks of feeling a bit worn out, Y-D's Ben Crabtree is downright perky. "My swing feels exquisite," he says. "I had good dreams last night, and that usually means good things." Brewster pitcher Scott Lonergan and his fellow Whitecaps are noticeably pumped up as well, and all expect the East Division series to be hotly contested.

The series opener is played before some 3000 fans at Red Wilson Field in Yarmouth, and Sox pitcher Daniel McCutchen quells his first-inning jitters in time to work out of a bases-loaded jam. In the bottom half of the inning, the Sox load bases, and Curreri forces in a run by taking a pitch off his foot. Ryan Rohlinger then doubles home two more, and the

Falmouth takes batting practice before playoff Game One.

Sox are off to the races. Before the afternoon is over, Curreri also clubs a two-run homer to right, and Crabtree gives life to his dream by hitting a two-run job of his own. The final score is 9-1, and a lot of the air has visibly gone out of the Brewster balloon.

Over in the West, Hyannis plays at Falmouth under the lights, and the resulting nail-biter is the polar opposite of the afternoon's blowout. Though the estimated 3500 people on hand watch the Mets hit four home runs, the Commodores still win 8-6, aided in part by four Hyannis errors and a passed ball. It's a see-saw battle the whole way through, as Falmouth jumps to a 3-0 lead in the third only to see Hyannis immediately answer back with a two-run dinger by Pat Reilly. League home run champion and MVP Daniel Carte then homers himself to push the Commodore lead to 4-2, and by the end of the seventh inning, the score is 7-3. But three outs later, the Mets trail by only one thanks to home runs by Joe Holland and Shane Robinson (a two-run blast). However, that's as close as they'll get, and they leave the ballpark knowing they must win the next two games in order to make the finals.

Playoff fever grips the throng at Red Wilson Field in Yarmouth.

It Takes Two to Clinch

All Cape League playoff series are best two out of three, so a second loss today by either Brewster or Hyannis will "send the club home." In the majors, this expression is used as a metaphor for the end of the season, for big league players usually return to their host cities to clean out their lockers before disappearing for the winter. However, "going home" here has a literal meaning, as that is precisely where most Cape Leaguers go the instant the last out is recorded.

At this point in the proceedings, nearly all are within days of having to report to their college programs, and since most went straight to the Cape from college back in June, they're eager to visit their families before starting the process all over again. So what happens today will determine what happens tomorrow, not only for the players, but for their host families and their general managers as well, who are affected just as greatly by any sudden end to the season.

The second game of each series takes place in the "other" ballpark to give the home fans of each team a chance to root their boys on to victory – and to give each franchise a chance to reap the financial windfall associated with a playoff appearance. Y-D president Bob Mayo says a post-season berth can make or break a club's ability to balance its books for the year because the crowds are both extra – that is, unanticipated – and extra large, and they result in additional donations and purchases of food and souvenirs. So while the playoffs mean extra duty for the team volunteers and executives, they are happy to be on duty, and the late-season excitement and enthusiasm they display do not stem only from the action on the field.

This afternoon's game in Brewster is a nip-and-tuck affair that bears little resemblance to yesterday's rout. In fact, the first run does not score until the fourth, when Y-D plates a runner on an error. Brewster then has a golden opportunity slip through its fingers when a bunt by Craig Cooper, intended to move along runners Gaby Sanchez at first and Andy Hunter at second, instead results in a fielder's choice for the first out, and an apparent RBI single instead generates the second when Sox center fielder Adam Davis throws out Hunter at the plate.

"That throw from Davis changed this game," Sox manager Scott Pickler later says. "It took the momentum away from them and gave it back to us again." Taking advantage, Y-D scores a run in each of the fifth and sixth innings, but gives one back in the seventh on an RBI single by Will Rhymes.

In the eighth, Y-D dodges another bullet and effectively ends Brewster's season: with Rhymes on third, J.B. Tucker smokes a rising line drive that pitcher Brett Harker somehow manages to spear, and since that is the third out of the inning, the rally dies, and the momentum shift seems complete. An inning later, it's official: Y-D wins 3-1 and sweeps into the championship round, where its opponent will be the winner of the Hyannis/Falmouth series that is resuming just as this game ends.

Roughly 1700 people jam into Hyannis' McKeon Park to see if the home-team Mets can force a Game Three, and they are rewarded by a return of the magic that pushed them past Cotuit and into the playoffs in the first place. The game is an excruciating 11-inning affair, and as may have been expected given events thus

> ### Ballyard Chatter
>
> "I figure you're only hitting .200, so I have 8 chances in 10 of getting you out – and since I have 4 pitches and you don't know which one you're getting, maybe I have 9 or 10!"
> – Scott Lonergan, Brewster pitcher

far, the hero is Mike Costanzo, who hits two home runs – one of them the game-winning blow – goes 4-for-6, scores four runs, and drives in two in Hyannis' 6-5 walk-off victory.

This outcome seems distinctly unlikely in the third, when Falmouth's Danny Perales hits a three-run homer to give the visitors a sudden and sizable lead. But in its typically scrappy fashion, Hyannis comes back with runs in the fifth, sixth, and seventh to take a 4-3 lead that stands up until the ninth, when Costanzo again switches from first base to the mound to close out the game. In an uncanny replay of the Cotuit game events, Falmouth takes the lead in what should have been their final at-bat; thanks to an error and a bases-loaded walk, the Mets now have to take their "last licks" on the wrong side of a 5-4 score.

Costanzo once more takes center stage and opens the inning with a single. After moving to second on a bunt, he scores on a two-out single to center by Mike Constantino, who becomes the third out trying to stretch his hit into a double. The crowd alternately roars and falls stone-silent as the inning unfolds, and when the dust finally settles, all anyone knows

Hyannis Met Mike Costanzo, here signing autographs at the All Star game.

is that this is some kind of ballgame!

The end comes suddenly in the form of a leadoff Costanzo home run in the eleventh, and it is almost anti-climactic, sealing as it does a game that features a combined 25 hits, 23 men left on base, eight walks, and four errors. But given the integral role Costanzo has played in determining the team's recent fortunes, it is fitting that he strikes the final blow. "What makes him a great player is his ability to deal with failure," says Hyannis manager King. "He just doesn't care about it," and that attitude is what keeps him going and has kept his team alive.

Third Time's the Charm

Less than 24 hours later, the Mets arrive in Falmouth for the third and deciding game of the series. Breathless and dis-believing after yesterday's affair, the players, fans, and team personnel all anticipate a much lower-key matchup for today, if for no other reason than everyone is just too tired to maintain the intensity of the night before. As it turns out, the almost

2900 people on hand aren't wrong, but it isn't until the last out is made that anyone feels the game is truly over.

Perhaps inspired by the presence of former Commodore and ex-major league catcher Steve Lombardozzi, who is on hand to throw out the first pitch (a chore actually performed by his son),

> ### Ballyard Chatter
>
> "All your dreams come alive here."
> — *Steve Lombardozzi, ex-Falmouth Commodore, Minnesota Twin, and Houston Astro*

Falmouth takes a 4-0 lead in the third on an infield single by Cliff Pennington and a three-run homer by the dangerous Daniel Carte. Always battling, Hyannis responds with a run in the sixth when Shane Robinson singles, steals second *and* third, and scores on an infield hit by Jay Miller. The Mets score again in the eighth when Mike Baxter singles and comes around to score on a double by Costanzo, who in typical aggressive fashion tries to take third on the throw home but is tagged out.

Though the home team still leads by a pair, the crowd is nervous because it is clear these Mets have no quit in them. But Falmouth plates an insurance run in its half of the eighth, and the game ends quietly a few minutes later with the final score of 5-2.

Strangely, the celebration is muted, partly because Pennington injured himself beating out his hit, but mostly because of the emotional toll these past few games have taken on the Falmouth squad. Sitting quietly in the dugout, the Commodores watch with a mixture of relief and envy as the Hyannis players receive their going-home travel money and bid farewell to their fans and to one another. They well understand just how close they came to being part of a good-bye scene themselves, and they know that they need only two more wins against a tough and rested Y-D club in order to go home as champions.

That Championship Feeling

Game One of the championship series takes place at Red Wilson Field in Yarmouth, where 3500 people squint into a cold wind that seems better suited for late September than mid-August. Storm clouds are gathering, and the day is growing prematurely dark. But the mood somehow is fitting, as the sensation that the seasons are passing matches exactly the reality before us: one way or another, the end of this weekend marks the end of the Cape League season, for if nothing else, NCAA regulations mandate that all its sanctioned leagues stop playing on or before August 15.

Falmouth is still without Pennington's services, but the team is confident in its ability to overcome adversity. So no one is particularly concerned when Ryan Rohlinger's double drives in Joe Anthonsen with two outs in the bottom of the first to give Y-D the early lead. And sure enough, the Commodores come right back to tie on a Brian Bogusevic leadoff home run in the second.

The Red Sox untie the score in the fourth, when Rohlinger walks, advances to third on a Frank Curreri single and a Nick Moresi fly ball, and scores on a throwing error by shortstop

Chris Lewis. Curreri takes third on the error but is nabbed trying to go home. It's an aggressive play that likely will be trained out of him if he progresses through the professional ranks, where he'll be conditioned to wait for the hit that drives him in. But it is necessary here, where the long ball is a luxury, every run counts, and the mantra is to "make them make the play!"

Falmouth seizes the lead in the fifth, when two singles and a two-out double by Danny Perales plates a pair. Slugger Daniel Carte is walked intentionally – the league MVP and home run champ draws three passes this day – and Y-D escapes when Mark Hamilton lines out to first. The Sox then scratch out the tying run in the sixth, when Moresi hits into a bases-loaded double play that allows Will Harris to score.

Two innings later, the teams demonstrate the veracity of Branch Rickey's long-ago statement that "baseball is a game of inches": Rohlinger slams a long drive to left, and Falmouth outfielder Jacoby Ellsbury very nearly hauls it in – but the ball has other ideas and instead clears the fence to give Y-D a one-run lead. However, Falmouth refuses to go quietly in the ninth, and worry soon creases the faces of the home-town fans.

Commodore second baseman Kevin Roberts opens the inning by grounding hard through third baseman Matt Ray and reaches on the error; Ellsbury then trades places with Roberts on a grounder, and Matt Antonelli flies harmlessly to center. With two men now out and two strikes on Danny Perales, the end seemingly is imminent. But pitcher Josh Faiola hits Perales with a pitch, and Carte strides to the plate with two on and fire in his eyes. The players stand in both dugouts, the fans jump to their feet, and virtually no one in the park is breathing.

And then, just like that, Carte flies to right to end it, and Y-D wins 4-3. Taking the first game in a short series like this is critical, for Falmouth now needs to sweep the next two in order to survive, while Y-D can afford to split the pair and still come out on top – and since the deciding game will be played in Yarmouth should it prove necessary, the Red Sox do hold a decided advantage.

The loss today is especially tough for the Commodores because they were fairly well spent after playing their hearts out three times against Hyannis, and they weren't able to score the much-needed pick-me-up that a hard-fought victory would have given them. Making matters worse, they also just learned that their missing sparkplug – Pennington – will not return to action. It's not easy, this championship stuff, but tomorrow's another day, and the game must go on.

No Tomorrow

The next day dawns so damp, dark, and windy that no one is willing to bet that Game Two can even be played. The forecast is grimly encouraging, but conditions here under the shoulder of Cape Cod are notoriously hard to predict. Team and league officials decide to play today for as long as the weather permits, and begin laying plans to make sure the field in Yarmouth is playable tomorrow should the third and final game be required. But what happens if neither game can be played? "We're screwed," commissioner Paul Galop says since there would then be no opportunity to get the game in before the NCAA's mandated "hard stop," and that's about as good a summary of the present mindset as there is.

The players, meanwhile, are busy with their pregame routines. Confident, loose, and ready to go home – or perhaps into the Arizona minor league system – Y-D's Frank Curreri says, "I'm going to swing out of my shoes tonight," and his teammate Ben Crabtree, who six weeks earlier earnestly described just how badly he wanted a championship ring, says

Y-D fans worry their boys home to victory against Falmouth in the finals.

"I can taste it now!" Crabtree's been hot lately and is starting behind the plate – Curreri will DH – and in keeping with his intensity, he's wearing a Superman T-shirt under his uniform. No one doubts that he would leap a tall building to get onto the field today!

Y-D slugger Matt LaPorta, on the other hand, is not especially keyed up for the game – in fact, he's not even in the dugout. Hurricane Charlie has just passed through his living room in Port Charlotte, Florida, and he's gone home to help clean up the mess and to tend to his family. So both teams now are missing a key contributor to their cause, and the others on the roster simply will have to take up the slack.

It's game time, and nearly 3300 people pack into Guv Fuller Field despite the bad weather. The conditions seem to be holding and may even be improving slightly, and the fans are ready for anything. Little do they know, that's exactly what they're going to get!

Y-D goes quietly in the first as Falmouth pitcher Jensen Lewis strikes out the side. Jacoby Ellsbury starts the Falmouth half of the inning with a walk, and – small ball to the rescue! – steals second, moves to third on a grounder, and scores on a Danny Perales fly ball. Daniel Carte then thrills the home crowd with a long double to left but is stranded there when Mark Hamilton flies to center.

The first sign that this may not be a typical night at the ballpark appears in the top of the second, when the Red Sox load the bases and manager Scott Pickler suddenly yells "Balk!

Balk!" and evacuates his third-base coaching box to plead his case before plate umpire Joe Peters. After checking with fellow umpires Joe Caraco and Tim Carey, Peters then allows it, and when he waves the runners ahead one base, the game is tied.

This decision triggers Falmouth manager Jeff Trundy to spring from his dugout to argue since it was Pickler, and not the umpires, who made the initial call. The ruling and the run naturally stand, but the tone for the game is set, and the commentary from both the Commodore bench and the Falmouth fans becomes loud and rather descriptive. Peace is restored when the last two Y-D batters strike out to end the inning, but Falmouth catcher Barry Gunther fires the ball into the dirt to signal his displeasure, and one has the distinct impression that the umpires' problems are only just beginning.

This feeling is confirmed just minutes later, when Commodore pitching coach Greg DiCenzo is ejected so suddenly that the Falmouth half of the inning hasn't yet even had time to begin. DiCenzo later says he was merely reminding the umpires to keep their focus on the players and the game, and he was as shocked as anyone when he was excused. But with the competitive juices flowing so freely, the umpires are giving very little slack, and it is clear that if they don't loosen up some, they – and we – will be in for a long night.

Play finally resumes, and Commodore DH Paul Christian temporarily calms the emotional seas by swatting a leadoff home run to again give the home team the lead. Shortstop

Chris Lewis follows with a single, and when Gunther is unable to lay down a bunt, catcher Crabtree picks Lewis off first. Gunther then fans, second baseman Kevin Roberts grounds out, and the momentum shifts back toward the Red Sox side of the field.

Crabtree continues his hot hitting in the Y-D fourth, when he fouls off five or six tough pitches and then doubles into the left-centerfield gap. Center fielder and erstwhile replacement player Ramon Glasgow then hits two long twisting fouls down the right field line before doubling to right-centerfield gap. Crabtree scores on the hit, and the game is now tied 2-2.

But this stasis is short-lived, as Hamilton and Chris Lewis both homer in the Falmouth fourth, and the Commodores surge ahead yet again. This time they build a two-run cushion, and with Jensen Lewis pitching his guts out (he will strike out 12 before he's lifted in the seventh), the most Y-D can muster from now until the ninth are a bunch of scattered singles. Now the momentum advantage lies with Falmouth, and this time the pendulum seems to be permanently stuck in their direction.

It's legitimately dark now, the sun having gone down, and Chris Leroux is now pitching for Falmouth. Glasgow opens the ninth by flying to left, and Y-D is down to its last two outs. Adam Davis then walks and is wild-pitched to second. Recognizing a turning point when they see one, both teams stand in their dugouts and crane for a view of the action, their fists clenched and jaws working in nervous anticipation. The fans too leap to their feet and roar when Joe Anthonsen walks and the Sox pull off a double steal that puts men on second and third. Will Harris then works a walk of his own to load the bases, and Curreri bounces a single to center that drives in two and ties the game.

Commodore fans are stunned into silence, Red Sox rooters erupt with excitement, and the Sox themselves rush to home plate to greet their returning heroes. Two quick outs then end the inning, but the damage has been done, and the fates, fickle as always, now seem aligned with Y-D.

Josh Faiola enters the game to pitch for the Sox and walks Carte to open the Commodore ninth. Curreri now is behind the dish (Crabtree has moved to first base, a lineup change that costs Y-D its DH), and when Carte takes off for second, Curreri throws a bullet to record the caught-stealing. Given the season Curreri has had, it seems only fitting that he should play an integral role on defense as well as offense, and the whole park applauds his effort.

An inning later, Faiola plays with fire when Gunther hits a one-out double, moves to third on a ground ball, and watches Ellsbury and Antonelli walk to load the bases. The crowd is on its feet again but is suspiciously silent as it holds its breath, but Perales lines out hard on a full count to right fielder Jim Rapoport, and Y-D again survives the threat. The fans wonder, How much more of this can we stand? and the players think, I'm running out of gas; we'd better win this soon!

It's the eleventh inning now, and Y-D's Joe Anthonsen answers the call by earning a leadoff walk and stealing second base. The play is very close, and the anger and frustration that has been building all game long finally boils over: Leroux is ejected while arguing the call, and Falmouth manager Jeff Trundy, livid at how quickly his pitcher was tossed, follows moments later after demanding an explanation. Even Y-D fans are disappointed with this turn of events since they – as everybody – want the outcome to be decided by plays on the field, and reprises of the early catcalls echo around the yard.

The new Falmouth pitcher is Kyle Young, and his first batter is P.J. Finigan, a late season replacement and a highly-regarded returnee from last year's Red Sox squad. Finigan is hitting for Faiola and beats out an infield hit. Curreri again rises to the occasion and sacrifices the runners to second and third. Young then walks Rohlinger intentionally to set up a force at any base, and perhaps an inning-ending double play. But before he does, he heaves a pitch well over his catcher's head, and Anthonsen scores to give Y-D a 5-4 lead. Finigan takes third on the wild pitch and scores a moment later, when Rohlinger puts his small-ball lessons to good use and executes a perfect suicide squeeze. Y-D gets two more on a Rapoport single and a Moresi homer, and after Crabtree singles, Glasgow grounds to short to bring the eventful inning to a close.

Brett Harker enters the game to close the game for Y-D, and immediately gives Falmouth hope by walking Carte to open the inning. But a double play clears the bases, and with two out, Christian walks. The fans cheer lustily but know the handwriting is on the wall, and when Chris Lewis flies out to right, the game ends, and Y-D secures its hard-fought 8-4 victory and the franchise's first Cape League championship since 1990.

The team and their fans rush onto the field and embrace while the Commodores look on, dejected but proud of the way they fought to the end. They know they nearly forced a "tomorrow" despite losing two of their key players, their pitching coach, and their manager. So while there may be no joy in Mudville [2], there is honor in Falmouth, and every soul in the park knows he or she has just seen a game for the ages.

Fare Thee Well

And then, just like that, the season ends, terminating with the abruptness of a washing machine lid slamming down. Barely minutes after battling to the point of exhaustion, the teams congratulate each other and repair to their respective outfield positions to huddle up as usual. But this time they are joined by the host families, team officials, and player parents in attendance, and even as the championship trophy is presented, the hugs and the tears begin.

Cries of "thanks for everything" and "we'll miss you" fill the air, promises are made to call and to write, photos are taken, and then, suddenly, there is nothing left to do. The visitors

---

[2] See *Casey at the Bat* by Ernest Lawrence Thayer.

climb on their bus and drive off. The home team changes clothes and disperses. The lights are switched off, darkness settles over the field, and another Cape League season passes into history.

The Y-D Red Sox hoist the club's first championship trophy in 14 years.

Y-D star – now Arizona Diamondbacks farmhand – Frank Curreri poses with the Cape League Championship Trophy.

Epilogue

The Circle of Cape League Life

The crowning of the league champion marks both an ending and a beginning as in the great circle of life: while the circumstances are not life and death, the players, host families, and team volunteers do mourn the passage of the season, even as they anticipate the next one soon to follow.

"There are plenty of tears at the good-bye," says Bourne general manager Mike Carrier, and the depth of the emotion on display has to be seen to be believed. It's hard to imagine that

Wareham players, host families, and team volunteers bid each other farewell following a special event at season's end.

a group of people could become so close after spending barely eight weeks together, but the angst of the impending team breakup is very real, and in many ways evokes the pain of long-ago summer romances. The difference is that the host families and team volunteers do this every single year, and they all will tell you that it never gets easier. "The hardest thing I have to do is go back and sort uniforms and cut travel checks," Hyannis Mets president Geoff Converse says, and with a rueful smile he gears up to do it again next year.

Reflections of the Season Past

For their part, the Merchant family of Wareham is glad to have housed a player for the first time this season, and host mom Sherri says she, her husband, and her son definitely plan to open their home again next year. "I owe much to the experience of being a host family," she writes. "Our lives are hectic with work schedules, sports, owning the businesses, and so on. But when we took on this venture, we found ourselves uniting in the ol' fashion family way."

One has the sense that the separation and transition back to "real life" is easier for the players than for the families and team personnel. In Merchant's words,

> Travis [Tully] will get home and move into his college home with his five new roommates, and will get back into his normal realm. For us, it's a bit tougher because our daily routine doesn't change, but we have a void in our home, not seeing his truck or hugging him or doing his laundry or hearing "MIZZZZZ MERCHANT, WHAT'CHA DOIN'?" from his room in the mornings!

This is not to say, however, that the players don't also feel the pangs and look back with affection and gratitude for their time on the Cape. Those who haven't signed with a professional team return to their schools and their baseball programs, tired but happy in the knowledge that they have made significant strides both as ballplayers and as people. Many of those with eligibility remaining are eager to return to the Cape next summer if they are invited, and some lucky ones already have been asked to do so.

Here, in their own words, are the perspectives of a few reflective souls who were kind enough to share their thoughts and were so eloquent in doing so that no editor could possibly improve upon them. That they all articulate such similar themes is entirely coincidental in that each responded independently to the same set of questions – but it also may be inevitable given how dedicated all Cape League participants are to making the experience so singularly rewarding.

Ben Crabtree

The most lasting impression I have of the Cape is of the people who made my summers memorable. When all is said and done, no one will remember who you played for or when you played; they will just remember the type of person you are and what you gave to the organization.

Personally, I had two very different summers on the Cape. My first was after my sophomore year in college, and I was coming to Brewster to play with the best of the best. I did not know how I would fit in or if I would truly belong, especially since I came from a mid-level college program. I felt like I had a lot to prove. In the end, though, I knew that I could play with the best of the best in the country.

My experience the next year was totally different simply because I had no roster spot coming up to the Cape. I took a temp contract with Cotuit just to get there, and when Y-D needed a catcher, I needed a place to play. So it worked out well.

Because I was coming off a season in which I had suffered a serious arm injury, I could not play as much or as well as I wanted, and in the long run I did not get drafted. The number one goal of any junior in college baseball is to get drafted and sign a pro contract. I did not get that opportunity, but I got another chance to play in the best league in the nation. Then I had to show that I was back from my injury. So both years on the Cape I had something to prove, to myself as well as to the powers to be in the baseball world.

The summer I spent with Y-D started with a host family in Centerville and then moved on to a host family in Yarmouth. The Zurns and the Hills really set the tone for the summer for me; I felt like I was at home and could just worry about playing and nothing else. Plus, they took me into their families and treated me like a family member. I will keep in contact with them for the rest of my life.

As for playing professional baseball, that has been the number one goal of my life. Last year was a serious disappointment because I had worked so hard, and it was rather tough to see it slip away. However, I know that if I stay healthy and keep working hard, I will get my chance. I may not get any money, but for me, it is all about the chance.

Whether I make it to the big leagues or not, I want to know in my heart that, in the end, I gave myself the opportunity to fulfill my goal. There are 1200 new players drafted every year, so the chances are slim that any one will make it. Yet every player has that one goal. The most amazing part of playing on the Cape is looking around and trying to figure out who the next major leaguer will be. Percentages say that I was on the field with a bunch of future big leaguers.

Chase Headley

My most lasting impression is definitely of the players I got the chance to play with and against. Who knows how many of these guys will be playing in the "Bigs" one day? It was a blast to go out and play every day against the best players in nation. It really gives you some perspective as to where you are as a player, and what you can do to improve yourself. I also made some friends that I think will be in touch for a long time. Also, the kindness of the host families on the Cape is something I have never experienced. My host family, Susan McCarty, her boyfriend Dan, and her son Brooks, are three of the best people I have had a chance to meet. They are family now. Without them, the summer would not have been nearly as great.

There were a couple of turning points that really changed the summer for me. I struggled when I first got to the Cape, and I mean big time. I was hitting below .175 for the first month of the season and worried about it consistently. Every at bat, I was putting pressure on myself to pull my average up. I finally just relaxed and realized I wasn't the only one struggling and did much better for the rest of the year.

The other major turning point was hitting my first home run. It came at Brewster a good month into the season, and it felt like I finally got the monkey off my back. I finally got some confidence and from that point on had much more success.

Will Rhymes

It's really hard to put my Cape experience into words. I guess what I kept thinking about on the long drive home was all the people I had met and how much I appreciated the town of Brewster for taking me in. One of the things I remember best was walking away from the field for the last time with my dad. Many fans were yelling at me as they were driving off, thanking me for playing at Brewster. The town really cares about the players, and supports them. They take pride in being a stepping-stone for future professional players.

I would have thought that my best memories would be of playing, but they are not. They are of my host family, the towns themselves, and the good times I had. I really don't remember any specifics about games except for the All-Star game and for my only home run. I feel so lucky to have been there, and so grateful for the people who gave me the chance. Every day

I was there I realized that it was probably the best day of my life, and each day I would correct myself and say, no, *this* is the best day of my life. I think it's rare that you can be aware at the time that you are living through the best time of your life. A lot of times we have to look back and say that. So it was a sad day when I drove across the bridge because I knew that it just didn't get any better than that.

I really don't know what my chances are of being drafted, though I know they are a lot better than they were before I played on the Cape. If I get drafted this year, I'll definitely go play pro ball. I'd be happy to put off med school for as long as I can!

Chris Robinson

Back to school now, almost half way done with the semester. Fall ball is over and now we are into our heavy lifting schedule ... I'm heading to Colombia with the Canadian National Team for the World Cup Qualifier at the end of October. Should be a good time. My roommate down there will be Chris Leroux, who played for Falmouth this summer (he is also Canadian). We play 14 games in just over two weeks, so it will be some good experience.

One of my lasting impressions is of meeting all the guys on the team and becoming such good friends. We had a very unique team filled with very unique individuals. There was never a dull moment, that's for sure! We had a lot of fun! Also I think meeting and becoming so close with my host family (the Blacks) will always be one of my best memories from the

Cape. I still talk to them weekly and am hoping to get back and visit sometime this year.

I think there was a point in the season where things just started to happen for me. Probably one-third of the way through, as soon as my parents came down, I began to see the ball better, get used to the pitching, and feel more confident. And once all of that happened, things fell into place for me. I was lucky that I had such a supportive host family that gave me something consistent to come home to every day after the game, whether it was a good or bad game. I strongly believe that the Blacks played a huge part in the success I had this summer, and for that I will be forever grateful.

As for turning pro, the draft is a very funning thing and is different for each individual player. I learned when I went through the process in high school that you can't control anything about it. Come June, if someone likes me enough to offer me a contract, then that's a bonus. When I started playing this game 16 years ago, I never thought that eventually someone would be paying me to play baseball anyway.

Cape League Players
in the Major Leagues

According to data compiled by Wareham Gatemen president and general manager John Wylde, 197 former Cape League players either were on a major league roster or on injured reserve for a major league team in 2004. This represents more than 15% of the 1200+ players overall who were entitled to pull on a big league jersey that season, a figure that is growing steadily year after year.

The names, teams, and draft standing of these players are listed below.

Player	Cape League Team, Year(s)	Draft Year	Draft Round	2004 Major League Team
David Aardsma	Falmouth '02	2003	1st	San Francisco
Russ Adams	Orleans '01	2002	1st	Toronto
Jon Adkins	Orleans '96	1998	9th	Chicago (AL)
Brian Anderson	Wareham '91-'92	1993	1st	Kansas City
Marlon Anderson	Wareham '94	1995	2nd	St. Louis
Scott Atchison	Wareham '96	1998	49th	Seattle
Garrett Atkins	Cotuit '98-'99	2000	5th	Colorado
Rich Aurilia	Hyannis '91	1992	24th	Seattle/San Diego
Jeff Bagwell	Chatham '87-'88	1989	4th	Houston
Paul Bako	Wareham '92	1993	5th	Chicago (NL)
Jason Bartlett	Harwich '00	2001	13th	Minnesota
Jason Bay	Chatham '99	2000	22nd	Pittsburgh
Mark Bellhorn	Cotuit '93	1995	2nd	Boston
Rigo Beltran	Brewster '90	1991	26th	Montreal
Kris Benson	Hyannis '94	1996	1st	Pittsburgh / NY (NL)
Brandon Berger	Cotuit '95	1996	14th	Kansas City
Dusty Bergman	Cotuit '98	1999	6th	Anaheim
Lance Berkman	Wareham '96	1997	1st	Houston
Larry Bigbie	Wareham '98	1999	1st	Baltimore
Craig Biggio	Y-D '86	1987	1st	Houston
Casey Blake	Hyannis '93	1996	7th	Cleveland
Joe Blanton	Bourne '01	2002	1st	Oakland
Geoff Blum	Brewster'93	1994	7th	Tampa Bay

Player	Cape League Team, Year(s)	Draft Year	Draft Round	2004 Major League Team
Aaron Boone (DL)	Orleans '93	1994	3rd	Cleveland
Darren Bragg	Cotuit '89	1991	22nd	San Diego/Cincinnati
Dewon Brazelton	Harwich '99	2001	1st	Tampa Bay
Eric Bruntlett	Cotuit '97	2000	9th	Houston
Brian Buchanan	Bre '93/ Hya '94	1995	2nd	San Diego / NY (NL)
Nate Bump	Cotuit '96	1998	1st	Florida
Jeromy Burnitz	Hyannis '88	1990	1st	Colorado
Pat Burrell	Hyannis '96	1998	1st	Philadelphia
David Bush	Chatham '00-'01	2002	2nd	Toronto
Mike Bynum	Hyannis '97-'98	1999	1st	San Diego
Eric Byrnes	Cha '95/ Hya '96-'97	1998	8th	Oakland
Shawn Camp	Chatham '96	1997	16th	Kansas City
Chris Capuano	Cot '97-'98 / Bou '99	1999	8th	Milwaukee
Sean Casey	Brewster '94	1995	2nd	Cincinnati
Kevin Cash	Falmouth '99	1999	ND	Toronto
Matt Cepicky	Chatham '98	1999	4th	Montreal
Randy Choate	Hyannis '96	1997	5th	Arizona
Jermaine Clark	Chatham '96	1997	5th	Cincinnati
Jeff Conine	Orleans '86	1987	58th	Florida
Lance Cormier	Wareham '00	2002	4th	Arizona
Jack Cressend	Cotuit '95-'96	1996	ND	Cleveland
David DeJesus	Bou '98 / Cha '99	2000	4th	Kansas City
Mark DeRosa	Bourne '95	1996	7th	Atlanta
Scott Downs	Y-D '96	1997	3rd	Montreal
Kelly Dransfeldt	Falmouth '94-'95	1996	4th	Chicago (AL)
Jason DuBois	Harwich '99	2000	14th	Chicago (NL)
Brandon Duckworth	Brewster '97	1997	ND	Houston
Jeff Duncan	Y-D '99	2000	7th	New York (NL)
Morgan Ensberg	Y-D '97	1998	9th	Houston
Matt Erickson	Wareham '96	1997	7th	Milwaukee
Scott Erickson	Cotuit '89	1989	4th	NY (NL) / Texas
Darin Erstad	Falmouth '93-'94	1995	1st	Anaheim
Nelson Figueroa	Wareham '94	1995	30th	Pittsburgh
John Flaherty	Harwich '87	1988	25th	New York (AL)
Randy Flores	Chatham '95	1997	9th	St. Louis
Josh Fogg	Hyannis '96	1998	3rd	Pittsburgh
John Franco	Cotuit '80	1981	5th	New York (NL)
Nomar Garciaparra	Orleans '93	1994	1st	Boston / Chicago (NL)

Player	Cape League Team, Year(s)	Draft Year	Draft Round	2004 Major League Team
Jody Gerut	Harwich '96-'97	1998	2nd	Cleveland
Doug Glanville	Wareham '90	1991	1st	Philadelphia
Ross Gload	Hyannis '95-'96	1997	13th	Chicago (AL)
Mike Gosling	Orleans '99	2001	2nd	Arizona
Jason Grabowski	Chatham '95-'96	1997	2nd	Los Angeles
Khalil Greene	Falmouth '99-'00	2002	1st	San Diego
Todd Greene	Y-D '92	1993	12th	Colorado
Seth Greisinger	Brewster '94-'95	1996	1st	Minnesota
Jeremy Griffiths	Wareham '98	1999	3rd	Houston
Jason Grilli	Cot '95 / Bre '96	1997	1st	Chicago (AL)
Matt Guerrier	Y-D '97	1999	10th	Minnesota
Jerry Hairston	Bou '96 / War '97	1997	11th	Baltimore
Brad Halsey	Chatham '01	2002	8th	New York (AL)
Aaron Harang	Cotuit '98	1999	6th	Cincinnati
Brandon Harris	Hyannis '00-'01	2001	5th	Chi (NL) / Montreal
Bo Hart	Cotuit '98	1999	33rd	St. Louis
Cory Hart	Brewster '96	1998	23rd	Milwaukee
Brad Hawpe	Y-D '99	2000	11th	Colorado
Todd Helton	Orleans '94	1995	1st	Colorado
Matt Herges	Brewster '90	1992	ND	San Francisco
Bobby Higginson	Bourne '91	1992	12th	Detroit
Eric Hinske	Hyannis '97	1998	17th	Toronto
Luke Hudson	Y-D '96	1998	4th	Cincinnati
Justin Huisman	Cotuit '99	2000	15th	Kansas City
Tim Hummel	Bou '98 / Orl '99	2000	2nd	Cincinnati
Brandon Inge	Bourne '97	1998	2nd	Detroit
Kevin Jarvis	Har '89 / Cot '90	1991	21st	Seattle / Colorado
Reed Johnson	Brewster '98	1999	7th	Toronto
Jim Journell (inactive)	Cotuit '98	1999	4th	St. Louis
Matt Kata	Chatham '97-'98	1999	9th	Arizona
Adam Kennedy	Falmouth '96	1997	1st	Anaheim
Jeff Kent	Cotuit '88	1989	20th	Houston
Jeff Keppinger	Orleans '00-'01	2001	4th	NY (NL)
Bobby Kielty	Brewster '98	1999	ND	Oakland
Mike Koplove	Chatham '97	1998	29th	Arizona
Mark Kotsay	Bourne '94	1996	1st	Oakland
Jason Lane	Hyannis '98	1999	6th	Houston
Justin Lehr	Y-D '97	1999	8th	Oakland

Player	Cape League Team, Year(s)	Draft Year	Draft Round	2004 Major League Team
Jeff Liefer	Chatham '95	1995	1st	Milwaukee
Todd Linden	Chatham '00	2001	1st	San Francisco
Braden Looper	Cotuit '94	1996	1st	NY (NL)
Javier Lopez	Falmouth '97	1998	4th	Colorado
Mickey Lopez	Orleans '94	1995	13th	Seattle
Mark Loretta	Falmouth '92	1993	7th	San Diego
Mike Lowell	Chatham '94	1995	20th	Florida
Mike MacDougal	Cot '97/Cha '98	1999	1st	Kansas City
Val Majewski	Falmouth '01	2002	3rd	Baltimore
Tino Martinez	Falmouth '86	1988	1st	Tampa Bay
Mike Matheny	Cotuit '89	1991	8th	St. Louis
Dave Maurer	Orleans '96	1997	11th	Toronto
Dave McCarty	Cotuit '89	1991	1st	Boston
Sam McConnell	Harwich '96	1997	11th	Atlanta
John McDonald	Bourne '95	1996	12th	Cleveland
Cody McKay	Y-D '94	1996	9th	St. Louis / Cincinnati
Dallas McPherson	Cotuit '00	2001	2nd	Anaheim
Jim Mecir	Falmouth '90	1991	3rd	Oakland
Adam Melhuse	Harwich '91	1993	13th	Oakland
Kevin Mench	Chatham '98	1999	4th	Texas
Lou Merloni	Bou '91 / Cot '92	1993	10th	Cleveland
Dan Meyer	Cotuit '01	2002	1st	Atlanta
Jason Michaels	Orleans '96	1998	4th	Philadelphia
Kevin Millar	Harwich '92	1993	ND	Boston
Eric Milton	Falmouth '95-'96	1996	1st	Philadelphia
Doug Mirabelli	Hyannis '90	1992	5th	Boston
Chad Moeller	Orleans '95	1996	7th	Milwaukee
Dustan Mohr	Wareham '96	1997	9th	San Francisco
Mike Mordecai	Y-D '88	1989	6th	Florida
Matt Morris	Hyannis '93	1995	1st	St. Louis
Chad Mottola	Brewster '91	1992	1st	Baltimore
Bill Mueller	Bourne '92	1993	15th	Boston
Mark Mulder	Bourne '97	1998	1st	Oakland
Mike Myers	Brewster '88-'89	1990	4th	Seattle / Boston
Denny Neagle (DL)	Y-D '88	1989	3rd	Colorado
Mike Neu	Brewster '98-'99	1999	29th	Florida
David Newhan	Y-D '93-'94	1995	17th	Baltimore
Lance Niekro (DL)	Orleans '99-'00	2000	2nd	San Francisco

Player	Cape League Team, Year(s)	Draft Year	Draft Round	2004 Major League Team
Greg Norton	Chatham '92	1993	2nd	Detroit
Augie Ojeda	Brewster '94	1996	13th	Minnesota
Russ Ortiz	Y-D '94	1995	4th	Atlanta
Josh Paul	Cotuit '95	1996	2nd	Anaheim
Jay Payton	Orleans '92-'93	1994	1st	San Diego
Carlos Pena	Har '96 / War '97	1998	1st	Detroit
Eduardo Perez	Brewster '89	1991	1st	Tampa Bay
Scott Proctor	Orl '96 / Hya '97	1998	5th	NY (AL)
J J Putz	Y-D '97 / Hya '98	1999	6th	Seattle
Robb Quinlan	Cotuit '97	1999	10th	Anaheim
Mike Remlinger	Wareham '87	1987	1st	Chicago (NL)
Brian Roberts	Chatham '98	1999	1st	Baltimore
David Ross	Brewster '96	1998	7th	Los Angeles
Aaron Rowand	Brewster '96-'97	1998	1st	Chicago (AL)
Kirk Saarloos	Cotuit '99	2001	3rd	Oakland
Tim Salmon	Cotuit '88	1989	3rd	Anaheim
Scott Schoeneweis	Chatham '93	1996	3rd	Chicago (AL)
Ben Sheets	War '98 / Orl '99	1999	1st	Milwaukee
Terrmel Sledge	Brewster '97	1999	8th	Montreal
J.T. Snow	Orleans '88	1989	5th	San Francisco
Earl Snyder	Wareham '96	1998	36th	Boston
Kyle Snyder (DL)	Chatham '98	1999	1st	Kansas City
Scott Spiezio	War '92 / Cot '93	1993	6th	Seattle
Denny Stark	Wareham '95	1996	4th	Colorado
Scott Strickland (DL)	Falmouth '96	1997	10th	New York (NL)
Cory Sullivan (DL)	Y-D '00	2001	7th	Colorado
Mark Sweeney	Cha '88 / Y-D '89-'90	1991	9th	Colorado
Nick Swisher	Wareham '00	2002	1st	Oakland
Brian Tallet (DL)	Wareham '97-'98	2000	2nd	Cleveland
Mark Teixeira	Orleans '99	2001	1st	Texas
Charles Thomas	Orleans '99	2000	19th	Atlanta
Frank Thomas	Orleans '88	1989	1st	Chicago (AL)
Rich Thompson	Cotuit '99	2000	6th	Kansas City
Mike Tonis	Brewster '98	2000	2nd	Kansas City
Andy Tracy	Orleans '94	1996	16th	Colorado
Chad Tracy	Orleans '00	2001	7th	Arizona
Chase Utley	Bre '98 / Cot '99	2000	1st	Philadelphia
Eric Valent	Cotuit '96	1998	1st	NY (NL)

Player	Cape League Team, Year(s)	Draft Year	Draft Round	2004 Major League Team
Jason Varitek	Hyannis '91/'93	1994	1st	Boston
Mo Vaughn (DL)	Wareham '87-'88	1989	1st	New York (NL)
Robin Ventura	Hyannis '87	1988	1st	Los Angeles
Ron Villone	Bourne '92	1992	1st	Seattle
Billy Wagner	Brewster '92	1993	1st	Philadelphia
Todd Walker	Brewster '92	1994	1st	Chicago (NL)
John Wasdin	Hyannis '92	1993	1st	Texas
Matt Watson (inactive)	Wareham '98	1999	16th	Oakland
Justin Wayne	Y-D '98	2000	1st	Florida
Jeff Weaver	Falmouth '97	1998	1st	Los Angeles
Kip Wells	Brewster '97	1998	1st	Pittsburgh
Turk Wendell	Falmouth '87	1988	5th	Colorado
Scott Williamson	Chatham '96	1997	9th	Boston
Dan Wilson	Cotuit '88	1990	1st	Seattle
Matt Wise	Y-D '95	1997	6th	Milwaukee
Danny Wright	Y-D '98	1999	2nd	Chicago (AL)
Kelly Wunsch	Orleans '92	1993	1st	Chicago (AL)
Kevin Youkilis	Bourne '00	2001	8th	Boston
Chris Young	Chatham '00	2000	3rd	Texas
Jason Young	Y-D '98	2000	2nd	Colorado
Adam Zinter	Harwich '88	1989	1st	Arizona
Barry Zito	Wareham '97-'98	1999	1st	Oakland

Cape League Players Drafted in 2004

Continuing the exercise, an accounting also was made of the Cape League players who were taken in Major League Baseball's 2004 first-year player draft. According to Sean Walsh and John Wylde, who compiled the list, a total of 186 Cape Leaguers were selected by major league clubs, including 125 players taken in the first 20 rounds.

The names, teams, and draft round of these players are presented below.

Round No.		Player	Pos.	CCBL Team	Drafted By
1	3	Phillip Humber	RHP	Y-D '03	NY (NL)
	4	Jeffrey Niemann	RHP	Harwich '03	Tampa Bay
	6	Jeremy Sowers	LHP	Wareham '02-'03	Cleveland
	8	Wade Townsend	RHP	Wareham '03	Baltimore
	13	Billy Bray	LHP	Orleans '03	Montreal
	16	David Purcey	LHP	Orleans '03	Toronto
	19	Chris Lambert	RHP	Chatham '03	St. Louis
	27	Taylor Tankersley	LHP	Brewster '02	Florida
	29	Matt Campbell	LHP	Y-D '02	Kansas City
Supplemental					
	31	J.P. Howell	LHP	Bou '02 / War '03	Kansas City
	32	Zach Jackson	LHP	Hyannis '03	Toronto
	34	Tyler Lumsden	LHP	Falmouth '01	Chicago (AL)
	36	Daniel Putnam	OF	Hyannis '02-'03	Oakland
2	42	Brett Smith	RHP	Orleans '02-'03	NY (AL)
	43	Eric Beattie	RHP	Bourne '03	Detroit
	44	Matt Durkin	RHP	Bourne '02	NY (NL)
	49	Mike Rogers	RHP	Y-D '02	Oakland
	52	Brian Bixler	SS	Brewster '03	Pittsburgh
	53	Wes Whisler	LHP	Y-D '02-'03	Chicago (AL)
	56	Jonathan Zeringue	OF	Orleans '03	Arizona
	57	Curtis Thigpen	C	Y-D '03	Toronto
	59	Donnie Lucy	C	Hyannis '02-'03	Chicago (AL)
	62	Jason Jaramillo	C	Orleans '03	Philadelphia
3	73	Jeff Frazier	OF	Chatham '03	Detroit

Round No.		Player	Pos.	CCBL Team	Drafted By
	79	Jeff Fiorentino	C	Cotuit '03	Cincinnati
	83	Adam Lind	1B	Wareham '03	Toronto
	86	Garrett Mock	RHP	Y-D '03	Arizona
	92	James Happ	LHP	Harwich '03	Philadelphia
	101	J.C. Holt	2B	Brewster '03	Atlanta
4	103	Collin Mahoney	RHP	Falmouth '02-'03	Detroit
	104	Aaron Hathaway	C	Brewster '03	NY (AL)
	106	Josh Baker	RHP	Wareham '03	Milwaukee
	110	Chris Iannetta	C	Chatham '02	Colorado
	111	Brandon Boggs	OF	Orleans '02-'03	Texas
	116	Ross Ohlendorf	RHP	Chatham '03	Arizona
	123	Robert Johnson	C	Y-D '03	Seattle
	126	Chris Shaver	LHP	Bourne '03	Chicago (NL)
	130	Clay Timpner	OF	Cotuit '03	San Francisco
5	132	Sean Kazmar	SS	Wareham '03	San Diego
	137	Mike Butia	OF	Bourne '03	Cleveland
	139	C.J. Smith	OF	Cotuit '03	Baltimore
	140	Matt Macri	3B	Brewster '03	Colorado
	141	Mike Nickeas	C	Wareham '02	Texas
	146	Cesar Nicolas	1B	Har '02 / Orl '03	Arizona
	147	Ryan Klosterman	OF	Chatham '03	Toronto
	148	Anthony Raglani	RHP	Chatham '03	Los Angeles
	155	Ryan Schroyer	C	Fal '01 / Orl '03	Boston
	158	Brad Davis	SS	Brewster '02	Florida
6	163	Brent Dlugach	SS	Hyannis '03	Detroit
	164	Ryan Coultas	SS	Y-D '02	NY (NL)
	174	Devin Ivany	C	Fal '02 / Bou '03	Montreal
	182	Sean Gamble	OF	Y-D '03	Philadelphia
	186	Tim LaY-Den	LHP	Cha '02 / Bou '03 / Cot '03	Chicago (NL)
	188	Brad McCann	3B	Harwich '02-'03	Florida
	190	Justin Hedrick	RHP	Harwich '03	San Francisco
	191	Clint Sammons	C	Cotuit '03	Atlanta
7	197	Marc Jecmen	RHP	Hyannis '02-'03	Cleveland
	201	Ben Harrison	OF	Hyannis '02-'03	Texas
	211	John Williams	LHP	Harwich '02	Minnesota
	212	John Hardy	SS	Cotuit '03	Philadelphia
8	224	Neil Jamison	RHP	Chatham '03	NY (AL)
	231	Mark Roberts	RHP	Brewster '02	Texas

Round No.		Player	Pos.	CCBL Team	Drafted By
9	245	Kyle Bono	RHP	Chatham '04	Boston
	247	Myron Leslie	3B	Orleans '02–'03	Oakland
	257	Chris Niesel	RHP	Falmouth '02–'03	Cleveland
	266	AJ Shappi	RHP	Hyannis '03	Arizona
	267	Joey Metropoulos	1B	Falmouth '02–'03	Toronto
	268	David Nicholson	2B	Y-D '03	Los Angeles
	270	Mike Parisi	RHP	Wareham '02	St. Louis
10	286	Steve Sollmann	2B	Y-D '02–'03	Milwaukee
	291	Justin Maxwell	OF	Bourne '03	Texas
	296	Steven Jackson	RHP	Fal. '01–'02	Arizona
	297	Brian Hall	2B	Y-D '01 / Hya '03	Toronto
	305	Steve Pearce	UTL	Cotuit '04	Boston
	306	Sam Fuld	OF	Hyannis '03	Chicago (NL)
11	312	Matt Varner	RHP	Falmouth '02–'03	San Diego
	323	Cliff Remole	1B	Bourne '03	Anaheim
	326	Darryl Lawhorn	OF	Falmouth '03	Arizona
	329	Garry Bakker	RHP	Cotuit '02–'03	Chicago (AL)
	330	Simon Williams	OF	Chatham '02	St. Louis
12	351	Kevin Ardoin	RHP	Y-D '03	Texas
	356	Richard Mercado	C	Hyannis '03	Arizona
	357	Eric Nielsen	OF	Cotuit '02–'03	Toronto
	360	Mark Worrell	RHP	Cotuit '03	St. Louis
	368	Jeff Gogal	LHP	Falmouth '03	Florida
	369	Rod Allen	OF	Orleans '02–'03	NY (AL)
13	378	Drew Anderson	2B	Falmouth '03	Cincinnati
	379	Denver Kitch	SS	Harwich '02	Baltimore
	383	Andrew Toussaint	2B	Bourne '03	Anaheim
	386	Antoan Richardson	OF	Orleans '04	Arizona
	395	Matt Ciaramella	OF	Y-D '03	Boston
	398	Steve Gendron	SS	Y-D '02	Florida
	400	Tom Martin	LHP	Falmouth '02	San Francisco
14	407	Jeff Sues	RHP	Falmouth '03	Cleveland
	409	Kyle Schmidt	RHP	Bourne '02–'03	Baltimore
	411	Tug Hulett	2B	Harwich '03	Texas
	423	Brent Johnson	OF	Falmouth '03	Seattle
	425	Robert Swindle	LHP	Harwich '03	Boston
	430	Eugene Espineli	LHP	Cotuit '02–'03	San Francisco
15	442	John Slone	C	Harwich '04	Pittsburgh
	444	Mike Wlodarczyk	LHP	Hyannis '04	Montreal

Round No.		Player	Pos.	CCBL Team	Drafted By
	447	Mike MacDonald	RHP	Chatham '02	Toronto
	452	Zac Cline	LHP	Harwich '02	Philadelphia
	460	Jeff Palumbo	SS	Bourne '03	San Francisco
16	476	Mark Reynolds	SS	Y-D '02 / Har '03	Arizona
	481	Matt Tolbert	SS	Bourne '02-'03	Minnesota
17	497	Marshall Szabo	3B	Y-D '03	Cleveland
	505	Adam Trent	RHP	Wareham '04	Kansas City
	506	Chris Carter	1B	Y-D '02-'03	Arizona
	510	Chris Noonan	LHP	Brewster '03	St. Louis
	518	Barry Gunther	C	Bourne '03	Florida
	520	Jordan Thomson	RHP	Brewster '03	San Francisco
18	522	Michael Moon	3B	Chatham '01-'02	San Diego
	530	Jeff Dragicevich	SS	Harwich '03	Colorado
	547	Jeremy SlaY-Den	OF	Falmouth '02-'03	Oakland
19	554	James Burt	1B	Brewster '03	New York (AL)
	560	Josh Newman	LHP	Harwich '02	Colorado
	573	Brandon Green	SS	Hyannis '02	Seattle
	575	Logan Sorensen	1B	Hyannis '02	Boston
	576	Micah Owings	OF/RHP	Bourne '04	Chicago (NL)
	577	Ryan Ruiz	SS	Falmouth '03	Oakland
20	589	Jonathan Tucker	2B	Har '02 / Hya '03	Baltimore
	601	Tim Lahey	C	Chatham '03	Minnesota
	606	Trey Taylor	LHP	Wareham '02-'03	Chicago (NL
	608	Rhett James	RHP	Orleans '03	Florida
21	621	Bobby Lenoir	SS	Orleans '03	Texas
	628	Justin Simmons	LHP	Hyannis '03	Los Angeles
	635	Chuck Jeroloman	SS	Harwich '03	Boston
	636	Will Fenton	RHP	Chatham '04	Chicago (NL)
	640	Simon Klink	3B	Hyannis '03	San Francisco
22	650	Stephen Edsall	RHP	Orleans '03	Colorado
	662	Anthony Buffone	3B	Orleans '03	Philadelphia
	664	Matt Brown	RHP	Bourne '01-'02	Houston
23	676	Tony Festa	3B	Harwich '02-'03	Milwaukee
	680	Jason Metzger	LHP	Orleans '02-'03	Colorado
24	707	Wyatt Toregas	C	Harwich '03	Cleveland
	716	Trey Hendricks	3B	Brewster '03	Arizona
25	732	Brian Burks	RHP	Wareham '02	San Diego
26	767	Justin Holmes	SS	Wareham '03	Cleveland
	776	Erik Schindewolf	2B	Falmouth '01-'02	Arizona

Round	No.	Player	Pos.	CCBL Team	Drafted By
27	795	Matt Goyen	LHP	Brewster '04	Tampa Bay
	805	Zane Carlson	RHP	Cha '01-'02-'03	Kansas City
	813	Aaron Trolia	RHP	Chatham '02	Seattle
28	845	Michael James	RHP	Harwich '03	Boston
	846	Jon Douillard	C	Wareham '02	Chicago (NL)
29	854	Michael Swindell	RHP	Orleans '03	NY (NL)
	855	Dan McCutchen	RHP	Y-D '04	Tampa Bay
	875	David Seccombe	RHP	Harwich '01	Boston
30	885	Aaron Walker	LHP	Y-D '03	Tampa Bay
	893	Alan Horne	RHP	Wareham '04	Anaheim
	895	Kris Krise	RHP	Brewster '03	Kansas City
	897	Corey Hahn	RHP	Hyannis '02	Toronto
	902	Kevin Shepard	LHP	Wareham '03	Philadelphia
	905	Drew Ehrlich	RHP	Brewster '01	Boston
31	936	Jesse Estrada	RHP	Orleans '03	Chicago (NL)
32	960	Austin Tubb	RHP	Hyannis '03	St. Louis
33	973	Kevin Brower	RHP	Cotuit '03	Detroit
	977	Paul Lubrano	LHP	Cotuit '03	Cleveland
34	1020	Brett Cooley	1B	Y-D '02	St. Louis
	1028	Jarrett Santos	RHP	Brewster '03	Florida
35	1055	Bo Lanier	RHP	Hyannis '04	Boston
	1060	Tim Grant	RHP	Bourne '03	San Francisco
36	1067	Jeff Kamrath	RHP	Brewster '02	Cleveland
37	1097	Blake Gill	C	Cotuit '03	Cleveland
	1102	Tim Rice	LHP	Chatham '03	Pittsburgh
	1104	Jamie Gant	RHP	Wareham '04	Montreal
	1106	Billy Lockin	SS	Orleans '03	Arizona
	1115	Glenn Swanson	LHP	Chatham '03	Boston
	1116	Michael Hyle	RHP	Cotuit '03	Chicago (NL)
39	1175	Zak Farkes	3B	Wareham '04	Boston
40	1200	Sean Dobson	OF	Bourne '03	St. Louis
41	1221	Clayton Jerome	RHP	Falmouth '03	Texas
	1226	Frank Curreri	C	Y-D '04	Arizona
42	1243	Jim Brauer	RHP	Y-D '01-'02-'03	New York (NL)
	1265	Ryan Morgan	3B	Bourne '02-'03	Chicago (NL)
43	1294	Adam Daniels	LHP	Cotuit '04	Chicago (NL)
44	1304	Phil Shirek	RHP	Harwich '03	Cleveland
	1307	Justin Keadle	RHP	Y-D '03	Colorado
	1323	Zane Green	OF	Cot '01 / Cha '03	Chicago (NL)

Round	No.	Player	Pos.	CCBL Team	Drafted By
45	1333	Tony Sipp	LHP	Wareham '03	Cleveland
	1344	Mike Hernandez	OF	Hya '04 / Ware '04	Los Angeles
	1354	Andrew Fiorenza	RHP	Hyannis '04	NY (AL)
46	1379	Tony Adler	RHP	Wareham '00	Houston
47	1409	Austin Easley	OF	Bourne '04	Boston
48	1423	J.T. LaFountain	C	Falmouth '03	Colorado
50	1495	Saunders Ramsey	RHP	Cotuit '04	Florida

Selected NCAA Summer Baseball
Administrative Regulations

Excerpted from NCAA Administrative Bylaw, Article 30

◊ Teams must be composed solely of amateur players.

◊ Players must be students of junior or senior colleges and have NCAA eligibility remaining.

◊ Coaches must come from a college, high school, or recognized amateur baseball team, and must not be employed by or paid by any professional baseball team or club.

◊ Players cannot play for a team coached or otherwise supervised by a coach from their own institution.

◊ No more than four players on the same team may be from the same Division I institution. All players must receive written permission from his school's director of athletics (or the director's official representative).

◊ Players cannot be assigned to a league or team by professional baseball clubs or organizations; however, they may be recommended to a league president or commissioner by Major League Baseball representatives.

◊ Players must have the opportunity to hold a real and necessary job, and will be compensated at the local going rate only for work actually performed.

◊ Teams may cover the cost of players' round-trip transportation (by direct route, up to the cost of coach air fare) from their home or college, and may pay for necessary travel, room, and board related to practice and game competition.

◊   No cash allowance or bonus shall be given to any player.

◊   All play, including league, non-league, and playoff competition, shall take place between June 1 (or the preceding Friday if June 1 falls on a Sunday or Monday) and August 15.

◊   A league all-star team may play a foreign country's national team, provided the foreign team's tour has been approved by USA Baseball, the league's schedule does not have to be changed, and the contest is held in the community of one of the league's teams.

◊   All teams shall use the NCAA's letter of commitment.

◊   No player, coach, or game official may use any form of tobacco during practices or games.

Extra Innings

Noah Timmer of Keene, New Hampshire, admires his autographed baseball.

(Top photo courtesy Tom McGinty Photography)

(Bottom photo courtesy Tom McGinty Photography)

(Photo top right courtesy Dan Dunn Collectables; center photo courtesy Bob Prew)

(Bottom photo courtesy Bill Bussiere)

(Top photo courtesy Bob Prew)

(Top photo courtesy Dan Dunn Collectables; bottom photo courtesy Tom McGinty Photography)

(Photo top right courtesy Tom McGinty Photography; bottom photo Sean Walsh/2004)

(Top photo ©2004, Cotuit Athletic Association. Photo by Rick Heath.)

(Center photo courtesy Bob Prew)

(Photo top left courtesy Bob Prew)

(Top photo courtesy Tom McGinty Photography; bottom photos courtesy Bob Prew)

(Top photo courtesy Bob Prew)

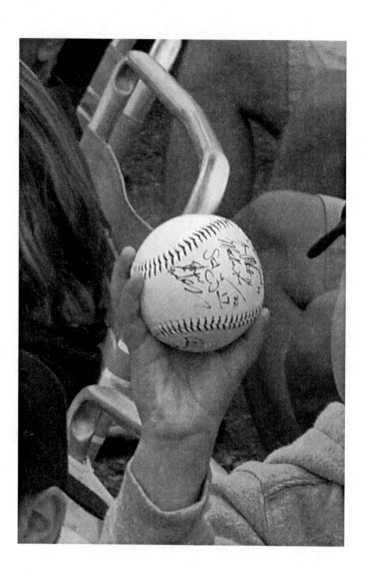

Acknowledgements

This book is the product of years of attending Cape League games and explaining to anyone who would listen just how great the experience is. It could not have been completed without the support and assistance of a large number of people around the league, on the teams, and in the community. These individuals generously opened their homes, their hearts, and their Rolodexes to help me understand the depth of their commitment and the breadth of their responsibilities, and to plug me into the essence and impact of their activities.

I could not possibly list everyone who shared their memories and experiences with me, but I am forever grateful to them all. Special thanks go to Cape League stalwart Bob Stead, who took the time to listen to the son of a friend of his neighbors and encouraged him to pursue his idea; to league president Judy Walden Scarafile, who kindly invited me to observe league's executive committee and general managers' meetings; to the committee members and the general managers themselves, who not only tolerated my presence but volunteered their insights for more than a year; to Dan Dunn, who enthusiastically opened his vault of memorabilia for background, flavor, and illustration; to the executives and volunteers associated with all 10 teams, as well as their players, managers, coaches, and announcers, for their steady flow of stories and perspectives.

To Glenn Matto, friend and fellow fan for nearly 20 years; to John Parker, Paula Boyle, and Sandra Churchill, colleagues, compadres, and editors to beat the band; to Tom McGinty, whose photographer's eye added a vital dimension to the work; and especially to my wife, Andrea, and our four boys, Nicholas, Christopher, Joshua, and Aidan, who supported me and encouraged me from first pitch to final out: I love you all.

One summer, two Red Sox championships: the Y-D and Boston trophies share the spotlight in Dennis, Massachusetts, in the winter of 2004. No fewer than 11 former Cape Leaguers helped the BoSox win their first World Series since 1918: Mark Bellhorn, Nomar Garciaparra, David McCarty, Kevin Millar, Doug Mirabelli, Bill Mueller, Mike Myers, Earl Snyder, Jason Varitek, Scott Williamson, and Kevin Youkilis. (Photo courtesy Bob Phillips)